TALKING WILD
WILDLIFE ON THE RADIO

ABOUT THE AUTHOR

Hailing from County Louth, Éanna Ní Lamhna is a self-styled expert on just about everything. She is best known for her environmental expertise as a broadcaster on both the television series *Creature Feature* and the radio programme *Mooney Goes Wild*. Her ability to bring her subject to life is legendary and her no-nonsense approach to romantic views about wildlife are well known. Originally a botanist, she is now a jack-of-all-trades lecturing in St Patrick's Teacher Training College and DIT, conducting Leaving Cert. ecology trips and inspiring environmental awareness in primary schools. She is married, with a husband and three children, and lives in Dublin.

TALKING WILD

WILDLIFE ON THE RADIO

ÉANNA NÍ LAMHNA

**TOWN
HOUSE
DUBLIN**

First published in 2002 by
TownHouse & CountryHouse Ltd
Trinity House
Charleston Road
Ranelagh
Dublin 6
Ireland

Reprinted 2002

© Éanna Ní Lamhna 2002

4 5 6 7 8 9 10

A CIP catalogue record for this book is available from the British Library.

ISBN: 1-86059-162-0

Cover design by Anu Design
Text design by Graham Thew Design
Illustrations by Christine Warner
Typeset by Graham Thew Design
Printed by Nørhaven Paperback A/S, Denmark

CONTENTS

Acknowledgements   8

1   Wildlife on the wireless   11

2   In the beginning   15

3   Drama in the garden – an everyday story of birdlife   23

4   Bird food – the à la carte approach   29

5   Miss Moffat's revenge – spiders   33

6   The terrible truth about bluebottles and flies   39

7   Sleepovers and holidays – coping with the cold   45

8   Bats in (and out of) the belfry   53

9   Wildlife isn't only for children   57

10 Adventure on Lambay Island   61

11 Introducing the crow family   65

12 Strange but true – bugs and their idiosyncrasies   77

13 Dandelions and other quare plants   83

14 Badgers and other carnivores   91

15 Lichens – a most peculiar coupling   101

16 Ageism – insect life cycles   107

17   Rabbits and hares and their unspeakable habits   115

18   Our own personal fauna   121

19   What'll it do to you?   133

20   The water police   141

21   Galling information   149

22   *An Dúlra Blasta* – edible wildlife   153

23   Your home as a wildlife habitat   159

24   Teaching teachers   167

25   Things that sting and things that don't – wasps,
         bees and ants   171

26   Maligned and misunderstood – who'd be an insect?   189

27   Sex and the single plant   195

28   Nature's weirdos – fungi   203

29   The ones St Patrick missed – amphibians and reptiles   211

30   Piseoga and folklore   225

31   Why did God make rats?   233

         Bibliography   239

I dedicate this book to
Vespula vulgaris, a much-maligned species.

◖ ACKNOWLEDGEMENTS

THIS BOOK WAS written in the middle of all the other work I do, with a hundred and one deadlines snapping at my heels, so I kept very quiet about it. Needless to remark there were fraught times when my wordprocessor seemed to have swallowed without trace every word I had written – so I wish to acknowledge the assistance of my long-suffering daughter Maebh, who miraculously retrieved it; long-suffering because, as she restored it so swiftly and so competently, I never managed to follow what exactly she did, again and again and again...

I also wish to acknowledge my husband John's ability to sleep while the keyboard tap-tapped away in the corner, thus assuaging any feelings of guilt I might otherwise have felt at keeping him awake into the small hours. I am grateful for the contribution made by the local chipper and the Chinese takeaway – their presence ensured that there was always food on the table.

I really want to acknowledge Richard Collins who cast his eye over the text on the look out for heresies. His advice has been invaluable and may well have saved me from the stake. Any heresies that may remain are my responsibility and cannot be blamed on anyone else.

ÉANNA NÍ LAMHNA
August 2002

CHAPTER ONE

WILDLIFE ON THE WIRELESS

UNTIL THE 1990s, wildlife programmes on the airwaves in Ireland were confined to television. Éamon de Buitléar and Gerrit van Gelderen had pioneered documentaries shot in Ireland with Irish wildlife featuring as the stars. Wildlife on the radio was not considered except in the form of earnest lectures or gardening information, although there was a series in the early 1950s (before my time) where J Ashton Freeman used to talk about wildlife and do bird mimicry.

But, like dancing on the wireless, it could be done. All that was needed was imagination to inspire it and a leap of faith to produce it. But how to go about it at the start of the 1990s? What did the ordinary person in Ireland at that time know about wildlife? What did they want to know? How much of it could they take at a time? How could you do it on the radio? The radio producer, Dick Warner, knew just the man for the job.

Enter Derek Mooney, a rising young presenter in RTÉ with a lively curiosity and a sense of the ridiculous. He was the person to know

the questions to ask, the questions that anyone at home might want to ask. The concept got going with a series on places where wildlife lived, called *Habitats*, and another, *The Nature Line*, answering queries written in by listeners. (This was in the days before e-mail.) But it was in May 1995 that the idea of a live interactive programme on wildlife was mooted by Derek Mooney and *Mooney Goes Wild* was born.

This programme would seek out fascinating nuggets of information about Irish wildlife, would keep abreast of current developments, would answer listeners' questions but, above anything else, would *not be boring*. Items were to be short and snappy, of the 'I never knew that' variety, and would not lecture the listeners. The format was to have Mooney as presenter, with a panel of so-called experts, Mooney being the arbiter of how interesting each piece was.

And it worked, beyond wildest expectations. The series has been running now since May 1995 and I have been on that panel of 'experts' since the beginning. The listenership has reached over 130,000 betimes and, as well as Derek, and latterly Richard Collins, I too have become irrevocably associated with it. 'Are you the woman on the radio? Every time I see a spider I think of you! I feel guilty when I kill creepy-crawlies now, thanks to you...' This sort of thing is the least of what I am accosted with when I venture out and open my mouth.

Wildlife radio has come of age in the last few years, thanks in no small measure to the Mooney show. Wildlife and nature now feature in mainstream broadcasting with Pat Kenny, Marian Finucane and especially Gerry Ryan on 2FM, regularly airing wildlife topics. Another important development has been the internet, with a profusion of websites developing on all sorts of nature topics and, here too, *Money Goes Wild* has fully availed of this medium. The broadcasting world is changing rapidly; where we go from here is anybody's guess.

But still the words have to come – when I stand up before an audience with my trusty slide projector, or when I am faced with a red light in the studio, I have to make the case for wildlife. So, what do I say? How do I go about it? I explain the world we live in, as it appears to me. I find the lives of other creatures fascinating and I try to convey this as convincingly as possible. And since you can't actually have my voice ringing in your ears all the time, here's the written version.

IN THE **BEGINNING**

THERE ACTUALLY WAS a beginning to wildlife in Ireland as we know it today, and that was 10,000 years ago at the end of the last Ice Age. Ireland had been covered with a layer of ice, a kilometre thick in places, for thousands of years prior to this and no plant, animal or person could live here. Global warming came about – I suppose even then that's what it was, although humans can't be blamed for that one – and caused temperatures to rise and the ice sheets began to melt. Now, this layer of ice had covered all the northern European countries, forcing the plants and animals to live in a much smaller Europe, the unfrozen southern half. The sea level was much lower too because of all the water held in the ice-sheets.

As the ice began to melt along its southern edge and retreat north-wards, bare countries were uncovered. Sea levels were so low that Ireland and Britain were not islands but were attached by land-bridges to each other and to mainland Europe. Faced with these wide spaces opening up, the plants and animals corralled for so long in southern Europe began to move northwards.

Those at the edge of the ice made the most progress. And it was a race against time – at least as far as Ireland was concerned. The ice was inexorably melting and the seas were getting deeper all the time. What could get to Ireland before the land-bridges were cut off? Hardy, speedy things had no trouble, and so cold-tolerant trees with wind-borne seeds were our first trees – think of willow and birch. Once we had trees, we had habitat for caterpillars and green-flies and so we had food and shelter for birds. Trees whose seeds were cunningly wrapped in juicy berries arrived, presumably origi-nally in the gut of gourmet birds – trees like mountain ash, holly, hawthorn, blackthorn, yew and elder. Finally the large trees, which formed the continuous leafy canopy in those woodlands slowly made their way here – oak, ash, elm and pine. But time was running out – the bridges were flooded. The beginning was over. The also-rans included trees like beech, which only made it to England (which lost its land-bridge to Europe much later), sycamore and horse-chestnut, which were still dallying in southern Europe and would now have to wait for millennia for entry visas.

And, of course, animals had the same conditions to endure. If you couldn't fly you'd have to walk, and coming by land was only possible when the land-bridges were still there. So we got stoats but for some reason not weasels; pygmy shrews but no other kind; wolves, bears and foxes; hares but no rabbits; red squirrels but no hedgehogs (they must still have been hibernating!); no dormice, no moles, no frogs, no snakes. Yes, snakes never got here. They were obviously disporting themselves on the Mediterranean shores when the ice began to melt, and by the time they slithered slowly north-wards to the Irish Sea, crossing was by ferry only. The English Channel formed much later than the Irish Sea, so the snakes did get as far as Britain and all the way up Europe to Sweden, but they never made it to Ireland – they were too slow getting off the starting blocks.

Earthworms weren't, though, and although their rate of movement can hardly be described as speedy, their starting line was much nearer the edge of the ice, as was the starting point for slugs and snails, all of which species are in abundant supply here.

Of course we only got a selection of what was available in Europe and, indeed, the selection there was no great shakes, compared to what was on offer at similar latitudes across the Atlantic in North America. This was because of the direction of the mountain ranges. In Europe they lie in an east–west direction – think of the Pyrenees and the Alps. During the Ice Age, as the weather got colder, the ice moved downwards over Europe and North America, pushing all before it in a southerly direction. But it was freezing on top of the mountains too and glaciers formed there and moved down the mountainsides. So the plants and animals fleeing the ice in Europe, came to the Pyrenees and the Alps covered in ice, with an ice sheet behind them forcing them southwards – surely the original quandary of being between a rock and a hard place! And many, many species became extinct.

But in North America, the Rockies and the Appalachians run north–south. The plants and the animals could move southwards with no bother and when the ice retreated they all went off northwards again. So today if you go to similar latitudes in North America, not only will you find different species, as you might expect on a different continent, but you will also find a much greater number of species as well.

If you were to fly in a helicopter over Ireland 8,000 years ago what would you see? Well, it would be an island, detached from all further supply of non-flying plant and animal species, but what exactly would you see from the air? You'd see 80 per cent of the country covered in forest – ash, hazel, sessile oak and elm on good soil; pedunculate oak and holly on acid soil; and the mountains covered in pine. The whole of the midlands would be one enormous lake. The melting ice had dumped its loads of sand and gravel in lines called eskers, where rivers once flowed under the ice, and these walls of sand and gravel had stopped the meltwater flowing away, making the low-lying central plain one large lake.

Come back in your helicopter 3,000 years later and a different scene would greet your eyes. The low-lying lakes had all filled in with vegetation, giving us the huge areas of raised bogs we had in the midlands until the advent of machinery, 5,000 years later, destroyed them all in sixty years.

The one thing you would not see in your first helicopter ride would have been much evidence of humans, but man was on the move too and no Irish Sea was going to deter him. Europeans had advanced from Palaeolithic (Early Stone Age) to Mesolithic (Mid-Stone Age) at this stage and it was Mesolithic man who first ventured across the sea to Ireland. (Scientists always use big words where short simple ones would do just as well: 'lithic' merely means stone, 'paleao' is old, 'meso' is middle and 'neo' is new.) The earliest evidence of human campsites in Ireland has been recorded from County Antrim from as long as 9,000 years ago. These were hunter–gatherers with primitive stone tools and they made little or no impact on the landscape. They couldn't cut down trees, so they had to travel by river and gather what they could to eat. Even then disposal of waste was an issue and landfill was the preferred option of disposal. How else can you explain the middens, some of which date back to this time – great heaps of shells carelessly tossed aside when they had finished dining in a favourite cooking spot?

Looking at these kitchen middens today, what strikes me is the size of the periwinkle shells they contain, many of them much bigger than those you commonly see on rocks nowadays. Middens also contain bones and the odd bit of pottery or jewellery that got lost at the feast. We think of these rubbish dumps from long ago as archae-ological treasure troves, but will that be the attitude to our landfill sites 5,000 years from now?

This happy state of affairs lasted until 5,000 years ago when a new coloniser made its way to our shores – Neolithic (New or Late Stone Age) man, the first farmers. Humans had got tired of this hunter–gatherer way of life and someone, probably a woman who had got fed up moving the tent to gather food somewhere else, thought, *'Why don't we make the plants grow beside us instead of always having to go and look for them?'* and gathered and sowed the seeds of the grasses most commonly eaten. The men used to disappear off on dangerous (and exciting) hunts, sometimes for weeks on end – not very convenient. A much better arrangement would be to have the animals too nearby, and then perhaps improvements could be made to the tent and it would be easier on the children – can't you just imagine it! This is quite possibly how domestication of animals came about. *£131,940/574.9415*

So successful did this farming way of life prove that populations expanded and more land had to be acquired – hence the movement of peoples across Europe and into Ireland. Even more remarkable was their behaviour when they got here. These were no primitive Mesolithic people – they were New Stone Age men with state-of-the-art stone tools and they knew how to remove trees. Being good ecologists, they knew that ash and hazel grew on the good soil, so they got rid of them first, to let the light in so that grass could grow and their cattle and sheep could graze.

And this was the beginning of the end for plants and animals that got in the way of progress. Some, like wolves and eagles, who were seen as the enemies of lambs and calves, were directly targeted. But it was also the end of the line for animals that needed large areas of untouched woodlands to live in – curtains for the wild boar and the woodpecker.

If the arrival of Neolithic man wasn't bad enough from wildlife's point of view, the weather deteriorated too – it got colder and wetter. It rained much more, particularly on the mountainsides, which were covered in pine forests. The saturated soil became an ideal habitat for *Sphagnum* moss, which grew over the roots of the trees, blocking the air from them, and so the pine trees died and the blanket bog grew up around them. Things don't rot in a bog, because it is too acidic and there's not enough oxygen, so the pine roots are there to this day – bog deal. The bogs grew over the early farmland cleared by the first Neolithic farmers too, as the excavations at the Céide Fields in north Mayo demonstrate.

Invaders, cold, rain – what else could happen? What else indeed but pestilence and disease? This time it was the elm tree that suffered, presumably with what we know today as Dutch elm disease. Within a short space of time most of the elms disappeared. We know this, because we can see that there is a sudden, huge drop in the amount of elm pollen that was trapped in the bogs at around this time (our bogs contain accurate accounts, in the form of layers of trapped pollen, of all the plants growing around them, their abundance and chronological order). It took nearly 400 years for the elm to recover its place in the native woodlands.

The helicopter ride 3,000 years ago (around 1000 BC) would show a different picture: the start of things to come, habitat destruction, species elimination and a new phenomenon – illegal immigrants. Because trade with Europe increased, stowaways came to Ireland on board the boats and ships, black rats and house mice came in food supplies, and brown rats, frogs and bank voles were to follow subsequently. And as man discovered metal, first bronze and then iron, tilling the soil became possible. You can write the rest of the script yourself. We can blame the Danes, the Normans, the Tudors, the Great Famine, the general perfidy of Albion, for the way the countryside was managed if we like, but the fact remains that, when we got our own hands on the tiller of government, the country was changed out of all recognition. By 1921 we had reduced our 80 per cent woodland to 1.5 per cent. We had introduced another hundred species of plants. Our bogs are now down to 3 per cent of land area from a one-time grand total of 16 per cent. Rabbits, hedgehogs, fallow deer and sika deer had been brought here to grace the menus and fill the cooking pots of the more adventurous.

And if you used to live in a forest – tough. You had two choices – become extinct or adapt. So capercaillies, who had no pine forest, took the first choice, while pine martens and jays just managed to cling on in the few remaining broad-leaved forests. Some of those who chose the second route, pragmatically took what was going. And what was going was hedgerow, miles and miles of linear woodland, taking up 1.5 per cent of the country. Many of the inhabitants of our garden hedges with which we are so familiar, such as robins and blackbirds, were originally woodland birds – surely a case of 'if you can't beat them, join them'.

Our hedgerows are extremely important habitats in the Ireland of today, an Ireland which has very little broad-leaved woodland. Although we are planting new woodlands, most of what we plant consists of coniferous trees, all the same species (foreign ones) and all the same age. So our original woodland flora and fauna are better off in old, long-established field hedges than in the new evergreen woodlands. We maintain that, generally speaking, we like wildlife. We enjoy looking at wild flowers and hearing the birds sing. Why, then, is the removal of the site hedge the first thing we do when we go to build ourselves a new house in a nice rural area? And why, oh why, do we replace it in so many instances with a hedge of evergreen Leyland cypress or – even worse – an ever-yellow one?

CHAPTER THREE

DRAMA IN THE GARDEN – AN EVERYDAY STORY OF BIRDLIFE

MANY OF OUR garden birds, which seem so tame and happy in our gardens, are actually dispossessed woodland birds. Take the robin, for example. Robins originally lived on woodland edges and, as woodlands diminished and hedgerows increased, they adapted to the change very successfully. In woodlands, communication between birds was by song because they couldn't see each other on account of all the trees and cover in the way and robins still sing, although they are wholly adapted to gardens now. Robins are unusual among songbirds in that both the male and female sing. (In most other bird species it is the male that does the singing.) Although, to be quite accurate, the female robin sings and holds territory only in the winter. She is more docile and quiet during the breeding season, as silence is the price she has to pay to get a mate. The male wouldn't like a female who sings!

We can start off the robin's story in winter. At this time, the robin visits the bird table - the shortage of food overcomes any xenophobic tendencies. But come spring and the lengthening day, the sap rises in the trees and a male robin's thoughts turn to love. But first there must be some land to make a good impression on the intended. Where else but your nice suburban garden?

So he stakes his claim and perches on the trees and bushes along the perimeter and advertises his eligibility with what is, to us, the most melodious song. The song also indicates to other male robins looking for territory the character and, indeed, the bottle of the singer. If another male robin thinks that he can take the singer on, he approaches. Our sitting tenant is outraged. He rushes towards the visitor with his body language screaming aggression. This, however, may not be enough to deter the intruder, and actual hand-to-hand (or claw-to-claw) combat may take place. Robins have been known to kill would-be land-grabbers.

The intruder dealt with, our hero resumes his song. Another robin appears. This time it is a female, checking out the local talent, having been mightily impressed with the song. But - would you believe it? - our hero doesn't know that she is female (both sexes look the same) and he rushes over again, full of aggro, to see off the intruder. Fortunately for the survival of the robin species, female robins know what sex they are and act accordingly. Instead of squaring up to the opera singer, she is suitably demure and submissive and puts your man completely off his stroke. She is tolerated in the furthest extremity of his territory.

It is not long, though, until one thing leads to another and soon he is enthusiastically showing her around the most desirable building sites on his property and feeding her choice titbits. She gets a good idea of what sort of husband he'll be, how good he'll be at finding food for a family and how sharp his eye is at spotting a secure nesting site. Once planning permission has been given, he's off helping with the collection of nest material from which she constructs a nest and fashions it to her body shape. And, of course, he is a very vigorous lover. Frequency of mating can range from once a day to twice an hour around the time of egg formation – he can walk the walk as well as talk the talk!

Robins can have a clutch of up to six eggs and the one-time neighbourhood thug makes a very dependable husband, feeding first herself and, later on, the babies with the creepy-crawly content of your garden. And, in a good year, the performance can be repeated twice and even three times over, with the same missus of course.

By the end of the summer, your robins could have at least ten babies, which together with the original parents, comes to twelve – a six-fold increase in robin population. The oldest ringed robin was thirteen years old when it died. Say yours are not trying for the *Guinness Book of Records* and live for only ten years, and all their offspring and their children set up home in your garden, how many robins will be in your garden at the end of those ten years? Increasing by a factor of six each year, you will start off with two, have twelve by the end of summer one, 72 at the end of the second year, 432 by the end of year three... and well over 120 million by the end of year ten! Well, will you? No, you will have two robins. And will there be a large heap of 120 million dead robins on your front lawn? No, of course not. The truth is that this amazing reproductive capacity of robins cannot possibly be fulfilled.

Go back to year one. With the best will in the world there is no way that twelve robins can find enough food in your garden over the winter (bearing in mind that in the same imaginary scenario there are twelve robins in the adjoining garden looking for food as well). They would die of hunger.

But things don't get to this stage, because most robins don't survive babyhood. They are almost all caught by predators in the inexperienced early days of flying. They are food for the next level in the food chain. It has to be – life is not a Walt Disney cartoon. But, somehow, while we might accept that a sparrowhawk could dine on one of your garden robins,' we are most outraged to see and hear the magpies do so. But at least they are hungry, and the robins are part of their food chain. They're not part of the food chain, though, for your beloved pussycat, stuffed to the gills with Kit-e-Kat or the like. He's not hungry, and he doesn't need to dine on baby robins. He just kills robins for the hell of it; he doesn't even eat them. More garden robins are killed by cats (unnecessary pets imposed on the food chain) than are ever killed by magpies. So, think of that if you own a cat before you open your mouth to deplore the marauding magpie.

In fact, the two robins in your garden at the end of the season are most likely to be one parent and one of the young – the luckiest, the most alert, the smartest youngster. In other words, it's the survival of the fittest. And off they go to separate territories for the winter and next spring the story begins all over again.

Of course, the same general principle applies to blackbirds, thrushes, wrens, blue-tits – whatever other birds are in your garden. All these birds are only concerned with their own species. Robins don't care how many blackbirds or thrushes come in. Great tits are only interested in other great tits. The number of bird species in your garden depends on the availability of cover, nesting sites and food – and indeed the absence of the resident predator, the cat, who can spend all day in the garden bird-watching as his dinner is assured by the tin-opener. At least the magpies have to patrol a much larger area and a well-hidden nest and careful, cautious parents can outwit them.

So, is your garden a good habitat for birds? You may think it is. You may be doing the divil and all putting out bread, hanging up

nuts in special feeders, even making those bird cakes that you get recipes for in wildlife magazines. But is this only moving the deck-chairs around on the *Titanic*? What have you done to the garden itself to ensure that it is suitable for birds? What grows there? What creepy-crawlies are welcome or at least tolerated? There's no sense in blitzing everything with weedkiller and pesticide and then putting out a few crumbs to salve your conscience. There's more to it than that, I'm afraid!

BIRD FOOD – THE À LA CARTE APPROACH

BIRDS ARE THE Public Relations Officers for wildlife. People like to see and hear them. They feel familiar with them. We have a manageable number of species here. You can recognise most of those you see and bird books are sufficiently available to make it easy to identify the more unusual ones. They herald the seasons: bird song – spring; swallows – the start of summer; cuckoos and corncrakes – summer surely; and geese, swans and waders enliven our winter days. We're proud of our status as being vital to the bird population of Europe and of having internationally important bird sites.

Much of our radio programme, and many of the phone calls to it, concern birds and their welfare. Irish people feed them assiduously in winter, being careful to buy the right kind of bird seed, free from pesticides. We nannyingly stop feeding them when they're rearing young, lest they might lazily fill their babies' crops with bread rather than high-protein insect food, but actually we *can* continue to feed birds in the summer if we want to. Chris Mead, the British expert on songbirds, said on our programme once that parent birds weren't eejits – that they were well able to work out the right food to give their babies (although he mightn't have put it quite like that).

And yet, and yet… why are we such two-faced hypocrites? Why do we poison all their food and then moan to the radio programme that the thrushes, say, are getting very scarce? How else would they be, when every slug and snail they consume has already been killed by you with a blue pellet?

In an ideal world, slugs and snails would form part of the normal variety of flora and fauna. They come out at night to feed (as many creatures do to avoid predators, in this case the birds). They are herbivores, so their numbers are controlled by the amount of food that is available to them. In a natural habitat – say, a woodland – there is a natural balance of species. Some of these are palatable to slugs and snails, but not so much that the place is overrun with them.

But in ecological terms, what is your garden? Like primeval man you have cleared away the naturally occurring vegetation, to grow particular things that you like either to see or to eat yourself. If any of the dispossessed, naturally occurring plants dare to try and return, you arrogantly refer to them as weeds and remove them by fair means or foul. You only want your carefully chosen selected plants. And, of course, whether by accident or design or just Murphy's Law, these carefully selected plants in the main are beloved of slugs and snails, who cannot believe their good luck to be living in the midst of such plenty. They go on to raise large families to share in the largesse, always being careful to feed only at night and to hide away when the light comes.

Birds, of course, haven't survived all these millions of years without learning a trick or two and thrushes in particular have specialised in snails. Step number one: get up early and nab them before they hide away. Step number two (and this is a thrush speciality): invest in opening equipment. It's hard to get a snail out of a shell if it has obstinately coiled itself inside, but thrushes have worked out how to do it. Hold it in your beak and bash it against a hard surface like a rock and eat the contents when it smashes open – simple! In fact, in areas like sand dunes where suitable stones are scarce, any available boulder is used by several thrushes and is called a 'thrush's anvil'. You can see the evidence in broken snail shells all round it. Although we have two thrushes, the song thrush and the mistle thrush – and, indeed, the blackbird which is also a thrush species – it is only the song thrush that has developed this technique. Gulls and grey crows drop sea-shells from on high to open them, but songbirds have never learned this trick.

But if you have upset the balance of nature by rearranging the plant species composition of the piece of land around your house (a preoccupation known as gardening), you don't want to hand over the fruits of your labours to voracious slugs and snails. Hence the little blue pellets. Slugs and snails are killed on the spot and thrushes can find them, no bother – even the late birds, never mind the early ones. Too many chemically killed snails can't be good for birds (would you like to eat them?) and, not surprisingly, the number of thrushes diminishes. And even if you conscientiously get up before dawn to bury the poisoned slug corpses by torchlight, you are still diminishing the amount of food available for birds in your garden.

If we consider tillage farming – another unnatural practice, if we look at it purely in ecological terms – the number of herbivorous insects that are encouraged by such monocultures is enormous. A whole field of wheat is Christmas and its birthday for anything that likes wheat, and such creepy-crawlies can reach great numbers if unchecked. The way to check them is considered to be by killing them with poisonous sprays. Consider the amount of crop sprays and pesticides that are sprayed over large areas of intensive

agriculture – too often the headlands around the field and even the hedge get a blast too – and the wonder is that we have any insects left at all anywhere for birds to feed on.

What to do? Come on, you can work it out for yourself. Prioritise. Snails and slugs don't eat everything, so select species for your garden accordingly. Provide hiding places for the slugs and snails yourself, such as old mats, even empty grapefruit halves, and evict the tenants in the morning, preferably into open space where the birds can see and grab them. Protect the delicate plants you can't wean yourself off with a mini-glasshouse made from a 2-litre clear plastic drink bottle (with the top cut off to let the rain in) Snails find it hard to get their foot over these. And organic slug killers, such as beer in a saucer, at least do not poison the rest of the food chain. Then you can enjoy your birds with a virtuous glow.

MISS MOFFAT'S REVENGE –
SPIDERS

LITTLE MISS MOFFAT has a lot to answer for. We're fed this nursery rhyme as children and, as a result of the autosuggestion, I'm sure many otherwise normal adults are reduced to the screaming heebie-jeebies by just the sight of a spider. Is this fear justified? Does it stand up to scrutiny? Of course not. Irish spiders are not only harmless, they are our friends and should not be screamed at.

There are, broadly speaking, two sorts of spiders in Ireland. There are the web-spinning spiders, which spin webs to catch food, and there are the hunting spiders, which hunt after their food. These latter can make webs too for nests and suchlike, but they don't catch food in them.

We are all well up enough on spiders to know that they are not insects – they have eight legs, not six as insects do, and so they are, technically, arachnids. But did you know that they have eight eyes too, arranged in a circle on the top of their heads? A sensible place to have eyes if you are watching out for attack from above from hungry birds.

Web-spinning spiders occur in many different groups, distinguished by the shape and complexity of the web they spin. But many of us must be familiar (if we have an eye in our heads at all) with the garden spider, an expert web-spinner, who seems to be especially obvious in the month of September. The spider itself, if you look closely at it, has a white cross on its back making it easy to identify.

Web-spinning is a matter of finding a good location and getting established. To describe it in basic terms, an invisible, sticky, flexible curtain has to be put in place on a highway that is hopefully frequented by lots of flies. The anchor lines must be dropped first. These are lines of good, strong, spider silk, so that the whole edifice has a firm foundation. From the centre, the spider spins out thin sticky strands, which are the trap. This fills the whole space allotted for the web and the spider sits at the side attached to the last silken strand and waits for a fly to blunder in. And when one does, it is the vibrations on the end of the strand attached to the spider that alert it to the presence of food.

Out it charges at once, across the web to the struggling victim who is stuck fast. A quick bite with a dash of venom to the hapless fly's neck and he is no more. He can be eaten on the spot by sucking out all the juicy insides or, if the spider is a trifle full, the fly can be embalmed in lots of new silk and hung up in the spider's larder for leaner times. The fly didn't have a chance from the moment it touched the web; the sticky silk quickly entrapped it. But did you ever wonder how spiders themselves don't get caught in their own webs? There are two reasons, actually. The main anchor lines of the web, substantial threads of silk, are not sticky strands and the spider knows to move along these highways. But what about when it gets to the struggling fly in the sticky bit? The spider has oily feet, which don't stick to the sticky strands, a bit like the way a plaster won't stick to your knee if you put ointment on the cut first.

This means that spiders don't get stuck in each other's webs either, but why would you want to go calling if your neighbour is a savage cannibal? Spiders – particularly females – have no problem eating other spiders that come their way. So if a dashing young spider's thoughts turn to love, should discretion be the better part of valour? Certainly the phrase 'faint heart never won fair lady' could have been coined for the Lothario spider out on the town. How to win the lady without becoming her dinner? Well, like any good suitor he must bring a gift when he comes calling. A nice juicy fly, particularly well wrapped in sticky web, fits the bill, and no courting spider would set off without this. Mating in most species normally involves an extremely close intimate encounter, but our hero really doesn't want to get too close. So in matters amorous, his interesting body design comes into its own. Male spiders can transfer their sperm to the ends of their palps – two antennae-like appendages on either sides of their heads – which literally gives them breathing space during a mating encounter.

So a spider out for a night on the town arms himself with a juicy present, arranges his personal toilette, and comes calling on the neighbouring web. He indicates to herself that he has arrived by vibrating the sticky silk in the web. She thinks that dinner has landed and rushes out to polish off the intruder. Our hero quickly thrusts the gift-wrapped fly at his ladylove and while she is distracted unwrapping the present, mates gingerly with her from as far away as possible, keeping her literally at palp's length. If he hasn't wrapped the present enough, or lingers too long in the love department, herself has no compunction gobbling him up. The adrenalin rush must be mighty.

Actually, it makes no difference to the survival of the species if the female eats the male after mating – in fact the extra protein will

come in handy for the ensuing egg laying – because the vital sperm and male genes have already been transferred. But our hero would like to live another day and is very concerned that he should manage a speedy departure. So it is true: female spiders do eat their husbands, but not always.

After all this drama, the female spins a special web and lays the eggs in it. She then leaves the young entirely to their own devices. They hatch out and grow into spiderlings still in the web nest. They are dispersed by an interesting type of explosive action if the nest is touched at a certain stage of development. The young have got bigger inside, the web nest is stretched to bursting point and any outside pressure at all – say, being investigated by a predator – causes the web to burst and the spiderlings to explode out. This ensures their wide dispersal, stops them eating each other and, of course, enables at least some of them to escape if the nest is attacked by predators.

The big black spiders you find under loose floorboards or at the back of the garden shed are hunting spiders. These come out at night and chase their prey – earwigs, beetles, woodlice, anything that will provide a meal – around the garden. And they hunt over the whole garden and the walls of the house, anywhere they can find food. They come in and out of the house through open windows with impunity. They do, that is, until they unfortunately enter the room in the house with the spider trap and indeed the room most likely to have the window open – the bathroom. They race around this room too, unknown to us, chasing prey in the wee small hours of the morning. That is until they have the bad luck to fall into the bath – for then they are trapped. They cannot climb up the slippery sheer sides and, of course, it is always a huge spider that gets trapped in the bath. The small ones seem to be light enough to scramble out.

What should you do about the situation when you are finished screaming? Cruel types wash them down the plughole. Food chain experts (or those who hate earwigs and woodlice even more) catch them in the tooth mug and empty them out the window. But you could spare yourself all the histrionics by simply putting the plug into the plughole. End of problem. This is not because it stops them coming up the plughole – they'd want to be equipped with sub-aqua gear to get through the water trap in the S-bend. No, it quite simply provides them with a ladder – if a spider falls in, it can climb up the chain attached to the plug and escape. A towel casually thrown over the edge would do the trick as well. Simple, really.

Spiders should be high on our list of friendly creepy-crawlies if only for the fact that bluebottles and houseflies are favourite items in their diet, and even I cannot think of a defence for the bluebottle.

None of the spiders in this country do us the slightest harm. Their jaws are not strong enough to bite us anyway deeply, and they haven't enough venom to kill us or do us any harm. They are tiny, really, in the world order of spiders. Our biggest spider would have a body size at most of about 20mm and its legs might be this length again; the whole thing, legs and all, would easily fit in the palm of your hand. The world's biggest spider is the Goliath tarantula. Its body size alone is 90mm, while its leg span can reach 250mm. In other words, were you to put this on your hand its body alone would completely cover your palm, while its legs would be the length of your fingers. Even this spider doesn't harm us: it lives in the northern part of South America and dines on snakes, toads and mice. You have to go to Australia for the really nasty spiders, such as the Sydney funnel-web spider or the red-back spider, or to the southern US for the black widow spider. So get a grip when you see a common-or-garden Irish spider. If this makes you feel bad, don't even think of how you might exist in a country where there are tarantulas!

THE **TERRIBLE TRUTH** ABOUT **BLUEBOTTLES** AND **FLIES**

AM I ON the side of all creepy-crawlies? Well, even I cannot think of anything good to say about bluebottles. Shall I give you the gory details?

Bluebottles are pretty typical insects – body in three parts, six legs, two wings. Standard enough arrangement. But did you ever notice how much walking a fly does? If you had wings, would you bother much with walking, when you could fly everywhere? So why do the flies do it? What are they up to? Well, flies have very interesting feet. First of all they have hooks on them so that they can grip on to any surface. They can walk up glass windows and walk upside-down on the ceiling. But they have something else on their feet – taste buds. And when you think about it, this is very useful. Our taste buds are on our tongues and if we want to taste anything we have to put it into our mouths, and spit it out again hastily if it proves to taste nasty. How convenient it would be just to touch it with your toe and declare it to be palatable or not.

So that's why flies walk, when they could be flying – they're tasting things. One minute it could be the dog's droppings outside – the next it could be your dinner or the piece of ham cooling on the sideboard. They're not particular where they put their germ-laden feet.

When they do find a piece of meat they fancy (and bluebottles in particular love meat), how are they going to eat it? How well equipped are they in the teeth department? Well, very poorly; actually, they have no teeth. Their tongue is like a rolled-up hollow tube in their mouth, for all the world like a paper party whistle, and they can only feed by sucking up liquid through this hollow tongue. So the meat must be liquefied before eating and they have the very solution to do it with – vomit. They vomit on the piece of meat, the strong acid in this quickly liquefies the surrounding meat, and then they slurp up the vomit and the surrounding meat. Yum. And, if they want a second mouthful, they repeat the process. Then you come along, shoo away the fly and eat the meat yourself. Not any more you won't!

But what if it is a huge piece of meat in the fly's mind? A pity to waste all this good food just because the fly can't eat it all now. Ever with an eye to the future and the survival of the species, the fly takes this opportunity to lay eggs on the meat, thus ensuring a supply of food for its offspring.

This whole phenomenon often only comes to people's attention when the business happens in a confined space. Say a bird falls out of a nest in the chimney and dies behind the blocked-up fireplace. Or a mouse dies under the hot-water cylinder in the hot press. (Did you know that there's a hollow under the cylinder where it can be trapped?) In both cases, from the bluebottle's point of view, there is a supply of meat going a-begging and it will quickly detect it as it begins to go off. Each female can lay up to a hundred eggs and the eggs quickly hatch out into fly maggots – fat white juicy grubs.

These grubs feast away on the dead flesh and, in the fullness of time, maybe a fortnight later, they metamorphose into adult bluebottles. They are attracted towards light, which comes through the opening the original egg-laying bluebottle entered through, and they all swarm out through this to the light. Then you come into your under-used sitting room or summer holiday home and are appalled by the hundreds of bluebottles swarming in the window – or dead if you haven't come in for some time. This will continue to happen in waves until all the meat is eaten off the dead jackdaw or mouse, or until you find it first and dispose of it.

Old birds' nests under the eaves, particularly starlings' nests, can attract greenbottles, which are vegetarian and feed on the nest material itself. However, these are no more welcome a sight in hundreds in your sitting room than are their carnivorous cousins the bluebottles. And, indeed, their buzzing sounds have inspired no poet (no verses about bluebottle-loud glades), but in truth add to our general disgust.

So flies are the dustbin men of nature. They naturally break down and use up waste. If we are untidy with our dustbins and refuse and dump everything in landfill sites, we shouldn't be amazed to see vast quantities of flies. Could they be harnessed to eat up the putrescible waste in a controlled situation and the juicy white maggots fed to ducks as part of our food chain? Just wondering! (In the light of the foregoing we should have the bunting out for the spiders.)

An interesting side effect, as it were, of all this is how certain plants have exploited the situation. Flesh-eating flies are carnivores and don't eat plants, so why would they visit them? And would plants want them anyway? Flowering plants have been most ingenious in the way in which they have evolved to ensure their survival. Plants produce pollen – the male cells – and these need to fall on the female part of the flower in order to form seeds. It is much better if it falls on the female part of another flower of the same species some distance away, than for inbreeding to happen in any individual flower. So some species of plants have evolved means whereby they inveigle meat-eating flies to do this job for them.

Rafflesia is one such flower. This is the largest flower in the world, it looks like a large leathery cabbage and it grows on the forest floor in the tropical rain forests of Asia. When it is fully open and its pollen is ripe and ready for business, it exudes a smell of rotting flesh, so much so that the natives of these parts call it the corpse flower. The flies smell it when it is open and flock there in their thousands. They walk all over it looking for the non-existent rotting meat that they can smell, and in doing so get covered in pollen. Eventually disillusioned, they fly off. But again they smell rotting meat – another open rafflesia flower – and off they go to inspect, covered in pollen from the previous flower. So the rafflesia achieves its objective and gets itself pollen from a different flower. Of course, some of the time the smell must be a real rotting animal or the flies wouldn't survive.

Mind you, you don't have to go to the tropical forests to observe this phenomenon. We have the same carry-on in our own woods in spring, admittedly on a smaller scale. The arum lily, a common spring woodland plant, has a most peculiar projectile emerging from its flowerhead, called the spathe. This spathe has a rotten smell which is attractive to flies who think it is meat. They fly to it and buzz around it. The smell seems to them to be coming up from below and they seek urgently along the length of the spathe for the food. The neck of the spathe is protected by a rim of stiff hairs, which only bend downwards, so the flies can get in, but they cannot get out.

Eventually some flies arrive on the scene who have already been in an earlier arum lily and, of course, they are covered in that lily's pollen – this is what our lily has been waiting for. Once these slow-learner flies, who have again fallen for the smell-but-no-food trick, come down the spathe and touch their pollen-covered bodies off the female part of the flower, fertilisation of our lily takes place. Now the stiff guard hairs can relax and all the entrapped flies can rise up and escape. They visit other nearby arum lilies, always hoping that this time the smell is of food and so they continue the pollination process.

You can verify that this process is happening in spring by sniffing an arum lily. Only some of us can smell the horrible smell – apparently we have to have a gene for this, and if we do we are quickly deterred. But if you don't have the gene and can't understand what horrible smell your fellow-sniffers are complaining of, give up trying at once. Don't be tempted to give an extra hard sniff or you'll get all the deranged flies stuck to the hairs of your own nostrils. Ah, the joys of fieldwork!

SLEEPOVERS AND HOLIDAYS – COPING WITH THE COLD

ONE OF THE problems with living in Ireland is how to get through the winter. Seasons of mist and mellow fruitfulness don't last that long and cold, bleak winter approaches. Hibernation – sleeping through it – seems an excellent idea. Why don't we all do it? We could rearrange Christmas.

Well, it's not simply a matter of going asleep. If we tried to go to sleep in November and sleep right through non-stop till March, we'd wake up dead from hunger and thirst! It's just not an option. So how can bats and hedgehogs do it? They're much thinner than we are. If it depended on layers of fat alone, we could all point out people who could hibernate for several winters on the trot. The trick is not the amount of stored fat *per se*, but the body's metabolic rate. Our rate of breathing and our heartbeat rate are indicators of how fast our metabolism is ticking over. And our bodies are ticking over very fast indeed. We need lots of food at regular intervals to keep going, as any parent of teenage boys can vouch for.

But if you could slow down the engine, the fuel would last much longer. Think of the car. A full tank of petrol would last ages if you were just idling the engine and listening to the radio. And this is what hibernating animals can do: they can slow down their metabolic rate phenomenally – to one heartbeat a minute, for example – and they can lower their body temperature, helping their supplies of fat last all winter. That is what hedgehogs do, and bats and frogs, and all those mated female insects.

And that is what squirrels don't do. Squirrels don't hibernate, I don't care what Enid Blyton says. Think about it. Why would they be collecting nuts and storing them away if they were going to be fast asleep all winter? You don't see hedgehogs collecting snails, or bats stashing away moths. They are truly asleep and food is of no interest.

But if you can't hibernate, what else could you do to get through the winter safely? You could go on your holidays to warmer climes – in a word, migrate. But you need some means of transport and, as we live on an island, our migrating creatures, the birds, depart by air. It hasn't always been clear where birds went in the wintertime. Several hundred years ago people were convinced that swallows dived down to the bottom of ponds and hibernated there. There is even written evidence of this, as people wrote of stories they'd heard from fishermen who had dragged up such hibernating swallows in their nets. Even then you couldn't believe everything you read in the papers.

Well, that was in the Middle Ages when we would not be surprised at such a lack of knowledge. But I remember giving a talk on wildlife to a public audience in north County Dublin in the mid-1970s. Among other things – many other things – I spoke of corncrakes and lamented the fact that, even then, fewer and fewer of them were getting here from Africa. And I was publicly corrected at the end of the lecture by a very knowledgeable man, who patronisingly pointed out that, while in the main the lecture was good, I couldn't surely be serious about corncrakes flying here from Africa. Sure didn't everyone know that corncrakes couldn't fly! And his companions in the hall nodded sagely in accord. What the eye don't see... and to be fair, corncrakes fly very little when they do get here in summer. The bird ringers have to resort to ground nets to catch them for ringing purposes. But they'd be a long time walking to Africa.

The swift must be at the other extreme. It cannot take off if it lands on the ground. So at home is it in the air, that it feeds, sleeps and mates on the wing. The only things you cannot do in the air if you are a swift is lay an egg and incubate it. So in they zoom to our urban eaves in mid-May, their screeches indicating that summer has finally arrived. They collect no nesting material but lay just two to three eggs on the soffit (which is under your eaves, in case you didn't know). It's a race against time to get the young one reared for the mid-August departure. If we have a wet, cold summer it's hard for the swift to collect enough food. Indeed, in bad weather they can go into a sort of torpor to conserve energy. This is a kind of mini-hibernation in summer and it saves energy until the weather improves and supplies of insects are available again.

There is actually an American bird called the poorwill which does indeed hibernate for the winter months in a hole in a tree. Ornithologists thought they were great to discover this and were somewhat taken aback to discover that the local Indian word for the bird meant 'the sleeper'. Imagine them thinking they could know more about local wildlife and its behaviour than the indigenous Indian tribes who had such respect for their environment!

The swiftlets that visit China and the Far East have the same sort of general lifestyle as our swifts. They too are aerial feeders but they do build nests. The building material is their own saliva, which hardens in contact with air, like dried egg-white and indeed, like egg-white, the nests are mainly protein. This being the case, the thrifty Chinese harvest them when the birds have departed and they form the chief ingredient of bird's nest soup. So now you know, it's a real bird's nest in the soup in the finest Chinese establishments. I wonder who first thought of eating them?

The cuckoo, I suppose, is the most fascinating of all our migrating birds. In a world devoid of interesting and exciting events, the arrival of the cuckoo each April was especially welcomed by country people. Like most species of birds, it is only the male who sings, in this case making the characteristic cuckoo sound. (The female merely makes a not-very-loud bubbling sound.) The male cuckoo sings like this to attract a mate only, as cuckoos are not into property and don't hold territory or build a nest. And while cuckoos, as a species, can lay their eggs in the nests of several species of birds – meadow pipits, dunnocks, larks and robins have all been recorded – any particular cuckoo will only lay eggs in the nests of the species she herself was reared in. However, it may well be a tall order to find, say, nine meadow pipits' nests. If she can't find the 'correct' nest she will lay in the nest of another species. But as the cuckoo's egg tends to match that of the foster mother, the egg laid in the 'wrong' nest may be noticed by the nest's owners and the game will be up.

Timing too is important. Consider this dilemma. You are a cuckoo in Africa dependent, say, on meadow pipits to rear your young. You have to get to Ireland, mate and be ready to lay your eggs just as the meadow pipit has laid hers, so that it becomes part of the meadow pipit's life. If we have an early spring in Ireland, the meadow pipits will have a head start and the breeding situation will be far advanced early in the year. The cuckoo is too late coming with her eggs. On the other hand, if she arrives and spring is late, will the nests be ready when it is time to lay the eggs? How does the cuckoo get the timing right? After all, there are no weather forecasts of the spring situation in Ireland available to them in Africa. Do they come early just to be sure to be here on time? Not if the old rhyme is to be believed:

If the cuckoo sings on a bare thorn
Sell your cow and buy some corn.

This rhyme would seem to indicate that spring is normally well advanced by the time the cuckoo arrives and sings; and only in bad, late springs are they here before the leaves are on the trees.

When things go well and they do lay, perhaps one egg in each of nine nests, there is nothing more to detain the cuckoo here. So off they go, in July, the first migrants to depart – for them the summer is over. What, then, of the progeny? Well, the cuckoo's egg hatches fairly smartly and the first thing the baby does is heave out all the rest of the contents of the nest, in other words the legitimate offspring of the meadow pipit or whoever is the foster bird. The baby cuckoo has a special groove on its wing for doing this – if anything touches this, the baby is stimulated to heave it out of the nest.

And the odd thing, to us, is that the foster-parent birds don't seem to notice or care. They carefully and industriously slave away all summer feeding the monstrous offspring. Can't you just imagine them showing off when they meet other meadow pipits about how big their child is compared to theirs – and indeed the other meadow pipits smiling knowingly behind their backs. But, of course, birds are not people and we cannot know this. The Irish names for the meadow pipit – *banaltra na cuaiche* (the cuckoo's nurse) and *giolla*

na cuaiche (the cuckoo's servant) – reflect the fact that it is the principal host species to cuckoos in Ireland.

It is really difficult to comprehend what happens next. Most youngsters, when they are reared, stretch their wings, declare the area to be a boring dump and fly away to the next parish. But what makes the baby cuckoo (who thinks he is a meadow pipit) decide to fly, not to the next parish, but to Africa? Uniquely of all our migrating birds, cuckoos do not return to Africa with their parents and other adult birds. They go on their own. How do they know where to go and indeed when they have arrived? We know that they are genetically programmed to do this, or hardwired if you like, but it is still incomprehensible.

Of course we also get winter migrants. Just as swallows and swifts leave a perfectly good Africa to breed in Ireland because the much longer day here in summer gives them more time to feed, other birds fly north to where there is light for twenty-four hours in mid-summer. Among these are the herbivorous geese and swans who cash in on the huge amounts of food available when the earth's deep freeze, the Arctic tundra, thaws out each summer. There is plenty of time to feed during the long, long days, but they need all this time to get the young fledged and away before the cold returns. In winter, when the days shorten alarmingly and the grass is covered with snow, the geese and the swans come back here with their new families.

This fact was observed long ago by astute country people sensitive to every change in their surroundings. But they wondered where the young came from. The geese headed out over the sea in April and came back in October with young. What land could there be out on the ocean? So, particularly in the case of the barnacle goose, people came up with an ingenious explanation: clearly, the young rose up out of the sea. This is not so far-fetched as might initially appear because, after all, the evidence was there for them to see on the beach after a severe storm. Timbers washed up from deep waters are often covered in black and white animals hanging down as it were by their heads from the timber itself. These animals are actually shellfish called goose barnacles. It didn't take much imagination for the people long ago to deduce that these grew up to be the black-and-white barnacle geese that arrived from over the ocean each year, and, of course, as the geese came from the sea, they were really fish and so could be eaten on the many days of abstinence from meat that were with us at the time. They were called the priest's fish – so interpret that any way you wish.

The Children of Lir were the migrating swans; probably the Whooper swans, given that they sang. Mute swans with orange bills do not migrate but breed here, and they do not sing either. They were eaten at great feasts, forming a dramatic centrepiece on the groaning food-laden tables, as the Tudor cookery books tell us. There are many myths and legends about swans – both in Ireland and in other European countries – inspired by their mysterious and, in those days, little-known migratory habits. It's a pity that we have to spoil these stories with the facts.

CHAPTER EIGHT

BATS IN (AND OUT OF) THE BELFRY

CAN WE BLAME Bram Stoker? Was it his book *Dracula* that gave bats such a bad name or had they it already? The way that bats emerge only when darkness has fallen and the skill that they have flying effortlessly in pitch darkness through heavily wooded areas without mishap must have seemed supernatural to our ancestors. Add to that the fact that they emerge from crypts, belfries, disused buildings and ruined castles, and really *Dracula* was only the icing on the cake for a creature with a sinister-seeming lifestyle already. But where did the expression 'as blind as a bat' come from? Catching moths at high speed in a woodland in pitch darkness is not the action of a blind creature! And did they ever fly into anyone's hair?

Bats are fascinating animals – the only true flying mammals. They can be divided into three groups based on their dining habits. There are the fruit-eating bats of the tropics, the insect-eating bats of the temperate regions and, yes, the blood-sucking bats of Central and

South America. And they all work under the cover of darkness.

Our insect-eating bats are true hibernators. They spend the winter in secure roosts where the temperature never reaches freezing, so places such as underground caves and basements and crypts are perfect. When spring is well established and insect populations are sufficiently large to provide a continuous series of meals, the bats wake up and move quarters. What was fine for sleeping through the worst of winter won't do at all for summer – particularly for the females, who now require maternity quarters. The attics of our inhabited dwelling houses are good places for this. They get nice and warm during the day and, quite often, suitable attics are surrounded by trees or located by a river where lots of insects can live. Often times, however, these nice suitable attics are parts of buildings whose lower floors are inhabited by householders who manifest an absurd fear of these creatures and ring radio programmes imploring us to tell them how to get rid of them. Would they really prefer clouds of midges and mosquitoes and moths (all of which are eaten by bats) whose caterpillars wreak havoc on their crops and vegetables? Apparently they do. But all our bat species are protected by law, and wilfully destroying them is an offence under the Wildlife Act.

Bats give birth to one young per year, after what appears to us to be a bizarre courtship. Some females can mate with several different males (that's not the bizarre bit) and can keep the sperm of each separate inside. She can then decide which sperm she will use to fertilise her egg when ovulation takes place, and it is not necessarily the first one. This has all been discovered by using genetic fingerprinting to determine the father of the child. Not that he hangs around to mind the youngster. The maternity ward – your attic – is a mother-and-baby unit only, with the babies home alone while the mother goes out to feed – or else she carries them with her.

Bats can catch moths in the blackest of moonless nights in the same way as sonar was used by the Americans to detect submarines at sea during the Second World War – in other words echo-location. The bat emits a sound at a very high frequency, inaudible to our ears. This then bounces off solid objects and is reflected back to the bat at a slightly lower pitch. The bat is able to build up a picture of the surroundings from the changes in sound. Moths and other nocturnal insects are detected in this way and the bat can ascertain where the insect is and whether it is coming or going. A swift swoop and another mouthful of food for the bat. Is it likely that such a creature, who hunts in swarms and never crashes into another bat, is likely to get entrapped in your hair? (Unless, of course, it is festooned with moths or your head is completely empty, so that the sound waves pass through uninterrupted.)

But all such reason vanishes when a bat enters a room. At a public function I attended where such an event took place, the hysteria was mighty. I remember getting a phone call not so long ago from the principal of a girls' school. She was in a state. A bat had come into the corridor overnight and was there next day when the girls came in. What would she do? It was at present resting on the wall high up at the window, but who knew, it could wake up and fly into somebody's hair at any minute. No amount of reassuring her that this would not happen had any effect. So, more to get rid of her than anything else, I suggested that perhaps it could be gently encouraged out of the open window with a tennis racquet. She said that she would get the male member of staff on the job and hung up. Fifteen minutes later she was back. He was afraid and wouldn't do it. So I suggested closing the corridor for the day if they must, leaving the window open and that the bat would fly out again when darkness came. When I heard her voice again on the phone the next day I nearly had a weakness, but it was just to thank me most

profusely for the advice – the bat was gone. Never, never again would a window be left open overnight.

Tropical fruit bats are dull creatures by comparison. They don't hibernate because their food supplies never dry up – there is always fruit available in the forest all year round. And they don't use echo-location because they are herbivores – they eat plants, which cannot escape and don't have to be hunted down. They also drink nectar from night-opening flowers. For example, they leave footprints in the form of black marks on bananas as they stand on the fruit to drink the nectar from the next row of opening flowers. These bats fulfil an important role in pollination and seed dispersal in the windless tropical jungles, but we are such fastidious consumers that we won't buy bananas with bats' footprints, and so growers have to cover the fruit with bags while they are still on the plant to keep the bats from marking them.

But, I suppose, the blood-sucking bats are the most fascinating of all. Yes, they do exist, in Central and South America, and they feed on the blood of mammals, such as cattle and goats. Very silent in flight and light in weight, they land upon the victim and inflict a painless bite into a vein and lap up the blood. Needless to say, they don't attack humans – needless to say because, of course, you won't believe me. The *Dracula* story is much more fascinating.

NINE

WILDLIFE ISN'T ONLY FOR CHILDREN

SOMETIMES I FEEL a certain empathy with whoever said, 'I like children, but I wouldn't eat a whole one.' This is when well-meaning folk dismiss wildlife matters with the remark, 'Wouldn't it be great for children to hear this?' As if that was all it was – entertainment for children. When pressed, they say that children will have a love of wildlife when they grow up if exposed to it as a child, and then drag them along on a cold, windy, wet day on a field trip arranged for adults. And of course, for the child, it is often boring. Children are fed on a diet of wildlife programmes on television and, as in every other aspect of life, what you see on television bears no resemblance to reality. I have long suspected this, looking at the BBC extravaganzas, but having been involved in making a series called *Creature Feature* I am now sure. On television you can always see the creature in great detail – no quick glimpse against the sunlight here. This is because it is illuminated to perfection by a lighting operator whose job it is to do just that. In the real world,

57

you are often peering into a gloomy hedge or getting a fleeting glance at creepy-crawlies scuttling away from under a stone you have just upturned.

And did you ever notice that the animals on television always do things as you watch? The butterfly opens and closes her wings, the bee packs pollen into the pollen sacs on her legs, the bird returns to the nest with a mouthful of worms, the dragonflies mate at that very instant. These are the edited highlights of hours and hours of filming, when for much of the time nothing at all happens. What you are likely to encounter on your field trip is a spider running away rather than one in the act of eating her husband, having just mated with him. No wonder the kids feel short-changed.

And how do they get all these lovely close-up shots of bluebottles or wasps? I'll tell you how: they use cameras the size of a biro and they keep the insects in the fridge. Insects move very slowly when they are cold. The minute they look like warming up and taking off, it's straight back into the fridge. A five-minute *Creature Feature* can take all day to shoot if the creature is alternating between the bright lights and the fridge and there's only one camera to cover all the angles. Not quite what the young *Creature Feature* fan expects when he is lured out on a field trip.

It's the grown-ups who urgently need the wildlife information. After all, who puts the nonsense into children's heads? Who tells them that worms are yucky and screams inexplicably at spiders, which any self-respecting infant in a pram would catch and examine as part of the rich kaleidoscope of life? Who thinks that earwigs go in your ear and that wasps' only aim in life is to sting us? Who thinks wildflowers are weeds and should be replaced with big showy aliens from the other side of the world? Adults, that's who!

So when I hear 'Wouldn't the childer love this?' I know what is really meant is that it is the adults who feel that they are only

learning now what they should have learnt as children. The main
target audience for wildlife programmes in this country should be
adults between the ages of forty and seventy. For, unless they learnt

it elsewhere or taught themselves, they received no environmental education through state schooling. We did have nature study on the national school curriculum that we inherited from the British at independence. And this stayed on the curriculum until the 1930s, when de Valera came into power with Fianna Fáil. He wanted much more Irish taught in schools and, for all practical purposes, got the extra time for it at the expense of nature study. It was still nominally on the curriculum, but low in the hierarchy of the subjects it was considered important to teach. It was to be 1971 and the *Curaclam Nua* (the first one) before environmental studies became mainstream in Irish primary schools again. So, if you were born around 1930, you went to school too late for nature study. Or if you had left primary school by 1971 (having been born around 1960), you emerged unburdened by any knowledge learned at school about the creepy-crawlies that inhabit the world with us.

By and large, who makes decisions about the country we live in? What is the average age of TDs, county councillors, city managers, chief planners, town engineers, ministers for the environment, fisheries, forestry, arts, heritage, agriculture? What age group has the most wealth and puts the most demands on our environment? I would bet they are mostly people who went to school in that nature-studyless period between about 1930 and 1971. No wonder they say kids should learn about the environment, as they certainly know little enough about it themselves. But the reality is that schoolchildren are learning about environmental matters and have been doing so in some fashion since 1971. They are gaining even more awareness now with the revised curriculum for primary schools and with biology being by far the most popular science subject among Leaving Cert students.

It's not just kids' stuff. It is very much all our business.

ADVENTURE
ON LAMBAY ISLAND

HAVING AN INTEREST in wildlife opens doors where, ordinarily, we would have no business knocking. When I was in college, I did postgraduate research on, among other things, salt marshes. There was one plant species, rock sea lavender, that occurred in considerable abundance on Malahide Island in north County Dublin and was part of the salt marsh community there. It seemed to occur rarely anywhere else on the east coast, according to the literature. However, there was an old record for it from Lambay Island, where it was reported as occurring on the sea cliffs. With the brashness of youth, I wondered could the Victorian botanist who described it mean the same species exactly as occurred on Malahide salt marsh? If so, why did it grow on a cliff instead of a muddy substrate? Maybe it was a different subspecies at least.

Lambay Island was then, and is still, privately owned. In the early 1970s, it belonged to Rupert Baring, Lord Revelstoke. To examine rock sea lavender on Lambay Island, I would have to get permission from him. No better woman. I wrote asking him if I could come to Lambay to further my academic studies on this plant. To my amazement, he had his secretary write back to say that I could come and that he would send his boat to Rogerstown to collect me and bring me out. As it happened, there was other business to be conducted that day, as I discovered when I met the local garda sergeant at Rogerstown. It was at the beginning of the revival of the Troubles in Northern Ireland and all guns were being taken in. Revelstoke, a man in his late sixties, duly arrived in the boat with his gun and collected me (and a horse, which had also appeared with a minder) from Rogerstown pier. On the way over, my flapping raincoat startled the horse, which looked for a moment as if it was going to jump overboard, causing consternation among the crew and the handler. But not Revelstoke, who continued to talk to me above the noise as if nothing was happening and it hadn't all been caused by my being too silly to do up my coat in the first place.

Upon arrival on the island, Revelstoke had business with the boat and told me to come up to the house in due course. The western side of the island, where the boat had landed, was all agricultural land – more of the good market-gardening soil of the adjacent mainland of Rush and Lusk – not much of botanical interest for me there. The cliffs were on the eastern side and on my way to them I passed the entrance to the house, which looked to me like a grey gothic pile. Upon knocking on the door, I was admitted by an elderly house-keeper of at least eighty years of age and brought in to his lordship, who was now in the library. I felt that I should tell him about the rock sea lavender which, after all, was why I was there.

He was more interested in telling me about the house, which was designed by Lutyens, he of the Memorial Garden to World War I in Islandbridge. He told me this between sorties out of the library and back in again for no apparent reason that I could see. What was I to do? I hadn't been asked to sit down, never mind offered a cup of tea. Surely as his invited guest... I then heard him asking me, upon his return from yet another unexplained short absence, if I would go upstairs with him to see the engraving on the fireplace in the bedroom, and off he went, leading the way, before I could consider my position. And, gentle reader, I went, believing his story about the fireplace, down the corridor, past the table with the bottle of Black and White and a half-filled glass, out of which he had another gulp as he passed (which explained the disappearances from the library). Up the superbly designed stairs to the bedroom. And there was a fireplace, a large white marble one, and on it engraved in Latin were words to the effect that in this room Calypso Baring – his sister, he informed me – was born. Then, without any further ado, we repaired downstairs again to the library.

I felt that I should leave at this point, while I was ahead, saying that I had to search the cliffs for the rock sea lavender before the boat took me back (or didn't take me back at all, it being his private boat). His parting words were that I probably wouldn't find it.

I didn't. The ecology of the place had changed since the plant was recorded and an enormous colony of herring and black-backed gulls covered all the grassy areas between me and the cliffs – a population explosion caused by the abundant feeding available directly inland at Baleally and Dunsink tipheads. They were not amused at being disturbed, and retaliated by dive-bombing me incessantly. Surveying the scene from a safe distance, I realised that the guano from the colony had changed the flora of the cliffs. Gone, too, was the reported puffin colony, forced out by the gulls, and, I concluded sadly, gone also was any possible site for the rock sea lavender. Revelstoke was right. But why had he let me come when he knew this?

I spent the afternoon looking at the rest of the island and talking

to the farm staff who lived in houses that could have come straight out of a Thomas Hardy novel. They only got to go ashore at his lordship's pleasure – usually once a month when they got paid. He wouldn't let them go any oftener because they got drunk and were difficult to get back. Talk about the pot calling the kettle black! He made sure that he had supplies of his own tipple on the island.

It mustn't have been payday, as I made the return trip to Rogerstown unaccompanied by any farm worker and hungry enough to eat a passing seagull on a bed of rock sea lavender.

INTRODUCING THE
CROW FAMILY

OBSERVING AND RECOGNISING the things around us requires a certain amount of interest, I suppose. Observant schoolchildren in parts of Dublin's inner city will be able to tell me the colour and make of the car I've arrived in and probably its number plate as well. The names of dinosaurs or Pokémon characters or pogs – remember pogs? – present no difficulties to the average eight year old obsessed with collecting them all (at his parents' expense). Why, then, when I ask them to look out the window and identify the very few species of birds visiting their school grounds, do they proclaim with great dismissiveness, 'crows'? When I ask which crow, I am looked at as if I wasn't all there and told that they are black crows (as if there was the possibility of white, blue or yellow ones as well).

We have seven different species of crow in this country and four of them in particular are well known to us all. The magpie is indeed a crow, which now seems to be ubiquitous, particularly in suburban areas. Hard to believe that it is a fairly recent visitor to Ireland, having arrived here only in the 1670s. A party of them were blown over in a storm from Wales and landed on the Wexford coast. At that time the country was reeling from the ravages of Cromwell and the Cromwellian plantation, and this new bird was associated with the hard times resulting from his campaigns here. Therefore it was considered exceedingly unlucky to see one, and that is believed, in this country, to be the origin of the rhyme, 'One for sorrow, two for joy, three for a girl and four for a boy' (although in fact that rhyme is also found in Britain, so it is unlikely that Cromwell's invasion of Ireland really had anything to do with it). They have increased and multiplied very successfully over the years and indeed it is very rare now to see just one.

Magpies are extremely clever birds and are able to adjust very well to new circumstances. They observe what is going on around them and exploit what they see to their own advantage. They eat a wide range of food and are always on the lookout for new sources of supply. In the old days, when people got their milk delivered in glass bottles, the magpies used to watch the blue tits hopping up on the bottles, piercing the foil cap and having a sup of milk. So they had a go too. Berating the milkman one payday for the fact that my milk bottles were overturned and spilled by the time I got up to take them in, he informed me that it was the magpies who were to blame. Being clumsier and heavier than the blue tits, they managed to make bigger holes in the cap and to upset the bottle during the milk-stealing proceedings. In any event, the matter resolved itself as milk bottles vanished (too costly, no demand, and so on). As I can hardly open their replacement, the tetrapak, without getting covered in milk, I would welcome an enterprising magpie who could pierce it with a swift jab of the beak, but so far evolution has not moved that fast.

Magpies are ever vigilant for sources of food. Looking out the upstairs window recently, I beheld a magpie's bottom on the outside window ledge. It was for all the world as if the magpie was mooning at me. It walked along the sill and then bent over, tail up, presenting me with a view of its well-feathered bottom. What could it be at? I went outside to look. There was the magpie bending over the edge of the windowsill to pick out the snails and other creepy-crawlies that were sheltering under the window while waiting for nightfall to launch further raids on the garden. The magpie was picking them off one by one and crunching them, shell and all. The thieving magpie indeed!

Do they steal rings and shiny objects and bring them back to their nest? Personally, I don't know – their nests are mainly inaccessible, built out of sticks high up in the trees. They have that reputation, certainly, but no shiny objects have been scientifically recorded in their nests. Magpies build early in the year so that their nestlings will be hatched out and ready for feeding with the eggs of the later-nesting songbirds in the area. But whatever about hiding away shiny objects, what about making your nest entirely out of shiny objects? The magpie that nested on the Georgian balcony of the INTO headquarters in Parnell Square in Dublin did just that.

It wasn't remarkable enough that the nest was built on a third-floor balcony instead of in a tall tree but, even more bizarrely, the nest was built out of wire coat-hangers with only the odd twig inter-spersed. The magpies must have found a source of discarded hangers, which were asking to be recycled. But – lack of obser-vation again – no one had ever seen the magpies arrive with the hangers. Did they carry them in their beaks or on their feet? Did they carry one between two? Were there any dresses attached? However they got them, they must have provided a mighty uncomfortable seat for Mrs Magpie as she sat on the eggs to hatch them. But hatch them

she did and the parents successfully bred and fledged several offspring in such an unlikely place. The occupiers of the building grew quite fond of them and missed them when they finally departed.

The problem with magpies really is their lack of sneakiness. They attack in the open in full voice and their killing of our baby songbirds is heart-rending to observe. Mind you, your own over-indulged cat can inflict even worse casualties on the bird population of your garden. They do it in a covert, sneaky fashion and just for the hell of it, as we know from television advertisements (which are never wrong) that nine out of ten cats prefer a particular variety of cat-food and so could not be hunting out of need and hunger at all.

The next two crows that we commonly see are the so-called 'black crows', the jackdaws and the rooks. People had no trouble distin-guishing between them in the old days: *préachán* is a jackdaw and *cág* is a rook. It seems to be the English word 'rook' that we have difficulty with, because, on being pressed, people do remember that jackdaws nest in chimneys and that it is the 'crows' that nest in trees. It's hard to be a jackdaw with a need to find a chimney to nest in, these days. Long ago, when fires were the only form of heating, the jackdaw had to know which chimney to select. Of course, the active everyday chimney pots were very recognisable and no sane jackdaw would try to build a nest in a smoking chimney. But how were they to know when the odd fire would be lit in the parlour, or when somebody would be sick and have a fire lit in the bedroom? It's not any easier nowadays, even though we rarely light fires at all, because now the chimney pots are guarded with wire 'witches' hats' to keep the jackdaws from nesting. And when they do find a suitable chimney pot, in a disused outhouse or wherever, their troubles are only beginning.

Think of it. Imagine trying to build a nest in a chimney pot – a circle with a ten-foot drop. You have to get just the right-sized stick to jam athwart the chimney opening, to act as a base for the nest. You must select this stick without any tape to measure it, find just the right one by chance (you've no tools to cut and shape it), and then carry it to the chimney and insert it in just the right position, all with no hands. The large bundle of sticks below in the fireplace is evidence of their enduring patience, as again and again the stick is not jammed at the right angle and it falls down below. The wonder of it is not that there are so many jackdaws' nests in chimneys, but that there are any at all.

I lived in a bedsitter once, in the 1970s, at the top of a house in Dublin. The big room had been converted into a kitchen, sitting room and bedroom all in one. The fireplace was blocked up, the heating being provided by a one-bar electric fire on a meter. I woke up with a start at three o'clock in the morning in the dead of winter to hear a knocking coming from the fireplace. I put on the light and looked. Yes, definitely there was something on the other side of that piece of plywood blocking up the fireplace, which was knocking intermittently on the wood. And of course, as in all good horror stories, outside the rain fell and the wind blew in gusts. At three in the morning, all reason departs. Memories of that scene in *Wuthering Heights*, when Catherine Earnshaw comes back to haunt the narrator with knockings on the window, came flooding back. And, yes, I got up and dressed in a hurry and left in terror to join a friend in another bedsitter, who let me in and reassured me – a friend in need is surely a pest. Next morning, of course, courage had returned and back I marched to the bedsitter and removed the plywood, an action uncontemplatable alone at three in the morning. And what was there? Nothing but a huge collection of sticks from jackdaws' nests over the years. The waste pipe from the kitchen sink had been routed through the wall of the disused fireplace and the wind blew through the poorly sealed hole that the pipe went through, rattling the sticks. We'd had an easterly wind – an unusual one for Dublin – the previous night and the gusts rattled the sticks intermittently. Did I feel a right eejit? It never bothered me after that. I was able to be an expert, without even going outdoors, on when the east wind blew. I'm still waiting to meet a real ghost.

We got a wonderful insight into the life of breeding jackdaws when a very small camera was placed in a chimney to record a breeding season for the programme *Jackie and Daw*. This camera, placed so that it focused on the nest itself, recorded all that happened over a season. Three eggs were laid; two hatched out one day and the third one on the following day. Thus it was that two of the nestlings were bigger than the third and managed to attract most of the feeding. We watched a situation that was totally the opposite to that in a human situation, in which the two strong ones got most of the food and the small youngest one, who could not reach up as far in the nest, got less food. In a human situation, the small delicate child would receive extra care from the parents, who would not allow the siblings to bully it to the extent of depriving it of food. But nature is red in tooth and claw and eventually the smallest one died. At least the others didn't eat it, although they did eat a dead chaffinch brought in by the adults some days earlier. It was finally removed by one of the adults. The other two grew stronger and livelier and we could see them testing their wings and leg muscles. Then one day they just flew away and never came back. As it was a fixed camera, it didn't follow them, so we never saw them again. With technical assistance from Vinnie Hyland of *Wild Ireland*, The programme, however, incorporating as it did radio, television and live internet streaming, won a Prix Europa award for Derek Mooney, its producer and presenter, in Berlin that year.

Rooks start building their nests on the first of March, unless of course it falls on a Sunday, when, like good Christians, they wait until Monday. And indeed the busy sounds of the industrious rooks are one of the signs of spring. They repair last year's nests, not baulking at stealing repair material from their neighbours' nests while the owners are absent. This leads to terrible wars of possession and accounts for much of the noise made at rookeries.

Rooks are the farmer's friends. They enthusiastically follow the plough with jackdaws and gulls, feasting on the wireworms and leatherjackets in the soil turned over by the plough. These invertebrates are very partial to grassroots (should they be the emblems of Fianna Fáil?) and will inflict much damage on the farmer's cereal crops later in the year if not removed. So the farmer welcomes such vigilant pest removers. They also feed on earthworms and you often see them probing with their bills in grassy fields, playing pitches and indeed golf fairways and greens in pursuit of a snack. But they will eat food that we put in their way and, like magpies, are very clever at adapting to circumstances.

When I was at primary school, we ate our lunches out in the playground, discarding crusts and gristly bits of filling that we didn't like. At one o'clock, the master blew the whistle to summon us in and we lined up in an orderly fashion in the school yard. At the same time, the rooks (and indeed the jackdaws) heard the whistle and came flying in to line up on the school wall. They had learnt that there would be uninterrupted snacks available when we were all marched in. Active recycling. And they still do this, though nowadays they respond to the school bell rather than the whistle (and no doubt they are wise to the fact that schools, having reached such a state of excellence as to be awarded the coveted Green Flag, are no good for a snack, for such schools would not dream of discarding unwanted pieces of lunch in the playground).

It's easy to distinguish rooks from jackdaws when they are together. The rooks are bigger with pale faces and big bills and glossy black feathers, whereas jackdaws are the smaller ones and they look really neat, as though they had just combed their feathers. In adult jackdaws, the back of the head is a greyish colour. Rooks have black eyes, but those of the jackdaw are pale white or pale blue, contributing to the characteristic personality of the bird. Two different species, both crows.

The other common crow is so well known that it has several familiar English names: the scald-crow, the grey crow, the hooded crow. This large bird is definitely a baddy in the eyes of sheep farmers whose sheep lamb out on the mountains, and it gives all other crows a bad name. Grey crows love mountains, the sea coast, rubbish dumps – in fact anywhere they can find a dead animal or offal lying about. They are well able to exploit the terrain and its occupants for food, most appallingly in some instances. These birds are carrion feeders, scavengers. They will eat dead things that they have not killed themselves, so they peck at lambs that have died of exposure and they eat the afterbirths of ewes discarded on the hillside after lambing. They will eat road kill. So, fair enough, they have a role in nature – waste disposal – revolting as it might seem to some of us.

But they don't stop at this. They attack sheep if the animal is lying on its back and helpless. They can pick out the eyes of living animals, leaving the distressed blind sheep to die of starvation. They can even poke holes in a sheep's abdomen and pull out its intestines and eat them while the sheep is stranded on its back. No wonder it is not protected under the Wildlife Act, although you do need a licence to get a gun to shoot it.

The raven, another of our crows, is a much more majestic bird. It resides too in uplands and mountainsides, but it is much scarcer

than the hooded crow. Its Irish name, *fiach dubh*, has been incorporated into many placenames (as indeed has that of the golden eagle – *iolar* – another former resident of wild mountainy places). Ravens are the first birds of the year to nest, seemingly stimulated into courting behaviour by the lengthening day after the winter solstice. And these ravens do not court their sweethearts with mere dawn birdsong, or flashing plumage. No, ravens put on dramatic aerial displays in the sky over large tracts of mountainside, to show would-be mates what masters of the sky they are. And when a suitably impressed female joins in the aerial antics he is stimulated to even greater feats, flying upside down and passing food to his potential bride.

Ravens are beautiful glossy birds with such black plumage that their name has been given to a particular colour of hair on humans. And this raven-black hair was a sign of great beauty in Irish folk tales, as was skin as white as snow and lips as red as blood. It sounds like a vampire to me, but then I never met Naoise, the lover of Deirdre of the Sorrows, who was described in these terms to Deirdre, before she had even met him. This picture was conjured up when herself and her wise woman encountered a raven one snowy morning eating something from which blood trickled on to the snow. Yuck.

Ravens were also considered to be birds of ill omen. Like the hooded crows, they feed on dead animals. Noah's one never came back to the ark after being sent out to see if the flood was over – too busy, no doubt, feasting on drowned non-ark occupants. Cú Chulainn was so ferocious a warrior that even when he was finally killed in battle his enemies could not be sure he was dead and were afraid to go near him. (It didn't help that he had tied himself to a pillar when he felt death approaching so that he would die standing, facing his enemies.) So who would approach him first? Even on his last legs Cú Chulainn was to be feared. It was only when the ultra-cautious raven landed on his shoulder that his enemies knew he was definitely dead. And so Cú Chulainn is depicted in the famous statue in the GPO in Dublin, upright, tied to a pillar with a raven perched on his shoulder. It sure beats a death mask anyway.

Our two other crows are much less well known, because the habitat where they live is uncommon. Jays are denizens of deciduous woodland. Much of our woodland fauna can be found in hedgerows but not the jay, whose distribution declined with defor-estation. They are particularly fond of acorns and so are to be found in oak woods and large parks where there is plentiful tree cover. They are like a small magpie in design, but are a completely different colour. They are mainly brown but with a most brilliant flash of blue on their wings. Their 'song' is one of the most raucous in the woodland.

The chough is probably the least well known of all our crows, confined as it is to coastal areas in the south and west of Ireland. Its Irish name is much more descriptive, *cág cos-dearg*, the red-legged crow. Choughs are about as big as jackdaws and have bright-red legs and bills. They are particularly well adapted to *machair* – uncommon flat sand dunes in the west of Ireland with close-cropped swards. These they probe with their bills for invertebrates of all sorts. If you want to see them, they nest, among other places, in that beached ship thrown up on the coast of Innisheer in the Aran Islands, well known for appearing in the opening shots of the *Father Ted* series as Craggy Island. Approach with extreme caution, because the wreck is there since the 1970s and is falling apart with rust. The choughs nest inside and if you stand well away and watch during the nesting season you will see them.

So there you are – seven species of crows and not one of them a blackbird. Blackbirds belong to another family entirely, the thrushes,

and share no characteristics other than perhaps colour with the crows. But confusingly in the rhyme 'Sing a song of sixpence', it is rooks that are meant by 'four-and-twenty blackbirds baked in a pie', not blackbirds. According to one of my cookery books, young rooks shot on leaving the nest are tender enough, but adult rooks should be treated like elderly pigeons for cooking purposes. I'll spare you the details of the recipes.

CHAPTER TWELVE

STRANGE BUT TRUE – BUGS AND THEIR IDIOSYNCRASIES

'**STRANGE BUT TRUE**' was the title of a section in the comics I used to read *fadó, fadó*. It described weird and wonderful creatures that lived in places I was never likely to visit. What I didn't know was that we have our own strange-but-true heroes at home, if only we had eyes to look.

Consider, for example, the cuckoo spit. This spit-like object appears on twigs and grass stems in the month of June. The cuckoo is also heard in the month of June. Therefore the excrescence on the twigs is the spit of the cuckoo clearing his throat before singing and between calls. QED.

But it's not, you know. Where did this ridiculous story start? Did anyone ever see the cuckoo coughing up golliers? Any cursory examination of the 'spit' will reveal that it is no such thing. It is more like froth or suds, and if you probe it sufficiently with your fingers

you will discover that it contains a small green insect with beautiful brown eyes that will walk slowly on your outstretched digit. This is an infant froghopper and is a perfect example of camouflage.

The froth is produced by the nymph froghopper itself, by blowing air into a liquid it exudes from its own body, to prevent it from drying out. Even more importantly, the froth disguises it from the all-seeing eyes of the ever-hungry birds who would consider the hapless young froghopper a very tasty morsel indeed. Birds don't read books (or listen to the radio), so they have never copped on really to this source of food. They don't seem to realise that the 'spit' contains an insect.

The insect continues its life cycle unchecked and, upon reaching adulthood, is able to acquire food by sucking the sap of leaves through its piercing mouth parts. A sudden shake of a well-leaved branch into a carefully held open upside-down umbrella will dislodge the adults feeding on the leaves and you can observe their jumping ability for yourself by poking their hindquarters with a judicious finger.

Enthusiastic shaking of well-leaved deciduous trees in summer may well also unseat shield bugs. These insects are so called because their backs resemble the Roman shields of long ago. Remember the rectangular ones, behind which the soldiers could shelter, shoulder to shoulder in a 'tortoise' position? Well, the shield bug has a hard back, complete with shoulders, and the species we have in Ireland are distinguished from each other by their different colours and the food plant on which they are found.

Another name for them is the stink bug, and this reflects a not very nice trait they exhibit – a form of selfishness, really. They are herbivores and feed on the leaves of trees, as do many other creepy-crawlies, as the contents of your umbrella/insect trap will reveal. But stink bugs are real *'mé féiners'* and instead of sharing their leaf with

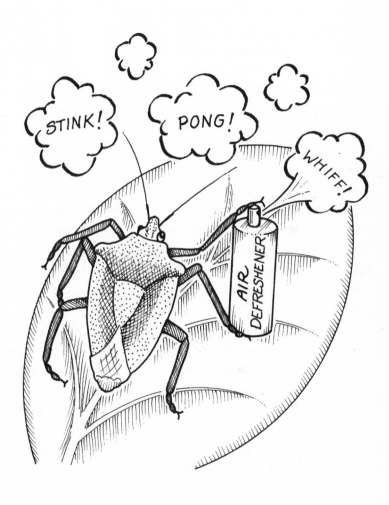

all comers, they secrete a foul-smelling scent all over it before commencing to dine, to deter any others from sharing the feast. Rather like a greedy child who licks all the buns on the plate before they can be stopped, so that nobody else will want one and they can have them all to themselves.

Maybugs are another interesting group of insects. The most dramatic of them is the cockchafer, a large brown insect that flies in the month of May – hence its name. It is the most frequent occupant of our postbag at that time of the year, as it seems to strike fear and terror into its beholders. Now, I will accept that it is quite a large insect, almost 3.5cm long, and that the males in particular have extraordinary antennae: they would put the old-fashioned chimney-top television aerials in the shade. But I don't think that it is its appearance alone that causes the terror. Its totally awkward way of flying also contributes to its bad impression. It comes out at night and blunders into houses through open windows and then it proceeds to crash into objects in its way, drawing unnecessary attention to itself. One mangled specimen I received came with the note, 'This got caught in the washing-up brush and somehow it died' – of shock, perhaps, at being at close quarters with the washing up. Or, more likely, it was bludgeoned to death by the same washing-up brush as a distraction from the dreary washing up.

But it was the cockchafer that provided us with one of our best answering-machine missions for the radio programme. This is a slot whereby a listener phones in with a query and leaves details on the answering machine. In return, they are rewarded with a visit from me to pronounce on the situation. On this occasion, the caller wanted a jumping egg identified – an insect egg all of 5mm long and shaped like a rugby ball that seemingly jumped of its own volition. Well, I jumped to it and went off to investigate immediately. The small, grey egg had been found under a hedge. It was the jumping that brought it to the observer's attention. It was now nestling in a plastic lunch box and was still jumping around. What was it – and why was it jumping?

Well 5mm, while quite small, is huge for an Irish insect egg. General insect books deal only with the adult insect, so descriptions of earlier stages in the life cycle are rarely accompanied by pictures. There were really only two likely suspects – one of the larger hawk-moths or our friend the maybug. The larger hawk-moths do lay eggs up to 5mm in size, but these are spherical rather than rugby ball-shaped and are mainly green anyway. The only one to lay a grey egg hasn't been recorded for Ireland. No, the cockchafer was the more likely. It lays grey, oval eggs. Inside, the infant insect develops into a comma-shaped larva with a brown head, which hatches out of the egg. It was the struggles of this larva to hatch that was causing the egg to leap about. The energy was in the creature inside – it wasn't the discovery of perpetual motion.

'Leave it to hatch and let me know what emerges,' I advised. When I hadn't heard for a fortnight I rang. Tragedy. The egg had stopped jumping and hadn't hatched. Once more a lightening dash to the house. Yes, the egg was well and truly still. So we got a very sharp knife and cut the egg in half, and boy had it a tough shell! Inside, sure enough, was the white larva of the cockchafer. But whether it was the temperature of the plastic box or the toughness of that particular shell, or its brief five seconds of fame on the wireless that halted the hatching process, we shall never know.

Cockchafer grubs do a lot of harm to garden plants, eating the roots, so the demise of one was no great catastrophe in the greater order of things. Still, I couldn't help feeling vaguely disappointed.

DANDELIONS AND OTHER QUARE PLANTS

LONG AGO WE had a much greater knowledge of plants than we have now. It stands to reason, of course: more of us lived in the country, for a start, and noticed the wild plants more. For many people, they were the only source of medicines, herbs to flavour food, dyes, poisons, magic potions – whatever. No wonder they were of interest generally. This is all gone now and people today are more inclined to be interested in birds (as a hobby) or creepy-crawlies (with a view to getting rid of them) than plants. But all that body of knowledge on plants hasn't gone away, you know, and sometimes it surfaces in unlikely places.

Take dandelions, for instance. Everyone knows the dandelion. It's one of the few plants I can put up on a slide in front of a general audience and everyone will answer correctly when I rhetorically ask, 'What's that?' And what they will also be able to tell me if I ask, particularly children, is what the bold word for dandelion is – pissy beds, wet-the-bed and other names in this vein. When asked to

elaborate they will solemnly tell me that I will wet the bed if I touch the plant, or maybe smell it, or maybe touch the juice that comes out of it. The story varies, and when I incredulously ask if this is true, they recant and say of course not. But it is actually true, dandelions will make you wet the bed, but only if you eat lots of dandelion leaves rather than just touch or smell them. It was very commonly used both as a salad vegetable and as a diuretic long ago. (The French, who will eat anything, still eat dandelion leaves with gusto in their salads and you commonly see bunches of *piss-en-lits* for sale in French vegetable markets.) We still have the name in common parlance here, but we've lost the association. Which is a great pity, because it seems that the dandelion was one of the most useful of wild plants.

It was in great demand as a healing plant. Eating the young leaves cleansed the blood and cured scurvy, but its great claim to fame was as a diuretic, as we've seen. Eating lots of leaves for this purpose was said to reduce blood pressure, and cure diseases of the heart and lungs. As dandelions contain lots of potassium, its use as a diuretic did not deplete the body of such essentials, but relieved kidney and urinary infections. The roots had their uses too. Extracts from these could remove kidney stones, and cure liver disease. And the white sap that comes from the dandelion was a definite destroyer of warts. Sometimes a mystique arose about this: the dandelions had to be gathered before dawn, the juice had to be applied nine mornings in a row, prayers had to be said while applying the juice, but one thing was sure – the warts went. An infusion of tea made from the boiled leaves could cure a sore throat or the measles. Chicken pox could even be cured but, in this case, a man had to give the dandelion medicine to a woman with the disease, while an infected man could only be cured if a woman gave the medicine.

And of course, in desperation, you could dry the roots and leaves and smoke them in your pipe if you had no tobacco, or dry, roast and grind the roots and pass it off as coffee. Mind you, you'd wonder about the coffee, as they also used to extract a magenta dye from the roots, but maybe roasting them got rid of the purple colour.

The Irish word for dandelion, *caisearbhán*, reflects its use and indeed taste, since it comes from *gas searbhán*, the bitter stem, referring to the bitter white 'milk' that it contains. Moneysharvan in County Derry means the bushy place of the dandelions. Here, as in other parts of Ireland, the dandelion was an important enough plant to christen a townland after it. Why is it called dandelion then? Well, the name came with the Normans from the French *dents de lion*, lion's teeth, reflecting the deeply toothed leaves it has. All this *béaloideas* in the common dandelion! If it were less common, I'm sure we'd have a lot more regard for it.

Plants were believed to have the cure of all sorts of diseases. In fact any plant with the word *wort* in its name shows that it had a medical use. Plants like ribwort, lungwort, St John's wort and stitchwort were used in medicine, as was ragwort, even though it contains poisons that are deadly to cattle. In fact, plants such as ribwort and lungwort got their names from the doctrine of signatures. This was a belief that, when God made the plants, he made some of them with cures in them for our ailments. In order to give us a clue as to what would cure what, he shaped the plants to look like the part of the body it would cure. Thus ribwort has prominent parallel veins on the back of the leaves, obviously resembling ribs. The lungwort is a large leafy lichen which, when placed flat on a table, looks like lungs, as portrayed in the old medical textbooks. Nipplewort and navelwort have appropriately shaped leaves as you might imagine. Liverwort is the name of a whole group of flat,

fern-type plants that grow in places kept wet with spray, such as near waterfalls, and must have reminded people of their livers. Many of these plants do have medicinal properties and, of course, the psychosomatic effect of taking a medicine guaranteed by God must have cured lots of people. But it takes more than a piece of lichen to counteract the effect of a lifetime of smoking, so don't be lulled into a false sense of security – they don't always work.

Woodlands were much more common in the old days and it is interesting to speculate on the names of some common woodland plants. Many of their English names came to us via the Normans, and later the English settlers, and reflect conditions in England when they got their names. For example, there was a famous magician (or wizard I suppose) in England called Robin or Robert and obviously he collected and used wild plants for his charms and spells. And so we have herb Robert, robin-run-the-hedge, enchanter's nightshade – all plants to which medical or even magical properties adhere, even today. Eating the leaves of the robin-run-the-hedge is said to make fat people thin, even though the same plant with the alternative name, goose grass, was fed to hens and geese to fatten them up. I suppose it goes to show that humans are not fowl.

There is a great deal of folklore and tradition associated with trees. The elder tree is a native species with fragrant creamy flowers in June and dark purple berries in autumn. It has extremely weak timber, more like pith, really, and it is called the boor tree in the northeastern part of Ireland. This is an Ulster-Scots name, meaning 'bore' tree or hollow tree, reflecting the lack of strength in the wood. The leaves have a horrible smell, particularly in spring, when they first unfold, and this is one of the results of it having being cursed by God. Now, you might well wonder why God would be going around cursing trees. The story is that the elder was the tree on which Judas hanged himself in despair after receiving the thirty pieces of silver for betraying Jesus. Now, to hang yourself in despair is such a terrible thing that God cursed the unfortunate elder tree. As a result, the timber of the tree is no longer strong enough to support a hanging person, its leaves smell awful and it is said that if someone is struck with a piece of an elder tree they will not grow any more. Another version of the reason it is cursed is the story that it was from elder that Christ's cross on Calvary was made. In any event, it is associated with bad luck, and no cradle or boat would ever have any part of it made from elder. The fact that the elder does not grow in the Holy Land is neither here nor there – why spoil a good story with the facts?

So associated is this tree with Judas that a particular dark-brown gelatinous fungus that appears on elder in October and November is called the Jew's ear. In spite of its uninviting appearance – it looks like folds of brown old jelly-like ears – it is good to eat and is much prized by the Chinese, who grow a similar species on oak palings and boil it for forty-five minutes in milk.

But the elder tree is only trotting after the hawthorn tree when it comes to folklore and tradition. The fact is that the hawthorn tree belongs to the little people and they are very proprietorial, particularly about lone hawthorn trees or groups of hawthorn trees in an isolated ring. To interfere with or cut down such trees is a recipe for disaster. Whoever would do so would suffer bad luck or die shortly after. We have spoken to people on the radio programme who knew people who cut down hawthorns and had terrible bad luck (although we never actually got to speak to any such individual directly – maybe that is part of the bad luck). In some parts of the country, it is considered the height of bad luck to bring the flowers indoors, but it is OK to put the same hawthorn flowers outside on the roof of the house on May Day. On the other hand, in other parts of the country, a branch of hawthorn broken off on Ascension

Thursday and brought into the house would protect the house and family from lightning, which of course was caused by the devil. The expression 'Cast no clout till May is out' was interpreted, when I was young, as meaning that you could not change into your summer clothes until the beginning of June. What it really means is that we should not shed our winter vests until the May blossom is out – in other words until the hawthorn is in bloom. We sweltered for an unnecessary three weeks. The fruit of the hawthorn was obviously not regarded very highly as we are told, 'When all fruit fails, welcome haw', a sentiment obviously not shared by thrushes and blackbirds.

The rowan tree or the mountain ash is also a tree with magic properties, but this time it is associated with good luck and the living. Witches feared it, so planting one near your house kept them away. It also protected milk and milk products against supernatural evil. It was kept in the byre to safeguard the cattle and put around the churn to ensure that the butter came during churning. The best switch for driving cattle was one cut from a rowan tree. It brought good luck in the currach when out fishing and one tied to a hound's collar would make it even fleeter of foot. It was at its most efficacious, however, in keeping the dead from rising – planted on a grave, it definitely ensured that whoever was down there stayed there.

In wooded Ireland in pre-Christian times, the trees were mainly deciduous and had lost their leaves by the middle of winter. So anything green was somehow magically holding on to life, plants like holly with shiny green leaves and red berries, and ivy with its lustrous leaves and black berries. These were surely symbols that the days would eventually stop getting shorter and that the sun would stop sinking lower in the sky. So when it was definite that the day was on the turn, say three days after the winter solstice, holly and ivy were brought into the house to celebrate this renewal. We still bring them indoors to this day, although with the Christianisation of those ancient pagan customs, we may no longer realise why.

Ivy had other value too. In ancient Roman times, it was the emblem of Bacchus, the god of drink, and was considered to protect against or even cure drunkenness. Here at home we had more use for it as a cure for headaches – a cap of ivy was made and placed on the sore head, on which pig slurry had first been placed. It was thought that the ivy would draw out the liquid that was causing the pain. Imagine the smell of such a treatment! You'd quickly declare yourself cured so that there'd be an end to it. Solpadeine, or aspirin, is surely a vast improvement. In fact, aspirin was originally found in the bark of the willow tree and is synthesised artificially now. A problem with aspirin is that it can cause stomach bleeding, but apparently there is also a drug that prevents this internal bleeding in the willow bark. So God knew what he was doing all right when he put such medicines there, but as he didn't leave any clues in the design of the bark, only the aspirin – salicylic acid – was extracted.

BADGERS AND OTHER CARNIVORES

THE MOST COMMON wild animal in Ireland is the badger, while rats and mice scarcely exist. This is the picture you would come away with, if you were gleaning your information on Irish mammals from the distribution maps produced by me in the Biological Records Centre in the 1980s. These maps were mainly composed of records sent in by observers, and often told more about the recorders than they did about the distribution of the animal species they were meant to be delineating.

In the case of the badger, observers felt that this was a wild animal worthy of reporting. They were all capable of identifying it correctly and indeed many of the records were of corpses killed on the road. Rats and mice, on the other hand, were not considered wild animals worthy of recording. Although I was sure that they were common and widespread throughout the country, I could not print distribution maps without records, and so the maps were very thinly populated indeed with dots indicating where they had been recorded.

The badger has been a resident species here since the last Ice Age ended and its ubiquity is reflected in the many placenames that contain its Irish name, *broc*. Badger setts in woodlands or under large hedges can have been there for many generations and reflect continued occupation in an area for many years. Badgers are creatures of habit and carry out the same actions day after day. They emerge from their setts after dusk slowly and cautiously, sniffing the wind carefully to avoid detection. They are omnivores, feeding on both vegetable and animal material. A favourite item in their diet is the earthworm and it has been reckoned that up to 40 per cent of their diet at times can be earthworms. The appearance of holes in gardens, lawns, fairways and greens, reported to us on the radio by irate gardeners and golfers, can often be ascribed to badgers on nightly forays for worms, but explaining who does it and why does not necessarily placate the owner of the garden with the holes dug out of it.

Badgers travel the same trails to and from their setts – trails that may have been used by many badger generations. They are also very brave animals, in our eyes at any rate, and will stand and fight any aggressor, as owners of dogs used for badger-baiting often learned to their cost. But travelling the same tracks and standing to face your enemy is not a good survival strategy if suddenly a new motorway is built over your nightly trail. And standing to face your enemy is unwise if the enemy with the shining eyes is a 10-tonne truck travelling at speed. No wonder so many of them are killed on the road. Thus, it is one small advance that, on new motorways that cross established badger territory (discovered during the Environmental Impact Study carried out before the site for the road is finally selected), underpasses are now being built to enable badgers to proceed on their way unmolested.

There are some improbable tales about badgers. Old people speak of two types of badger – the dog badger, which is a carnivore, and the pig badger, which is a herbivore and has a pink nose. The pig badger is the one to locate if the woman of the house has just given birth. In the old days, when confinements were at home, the mother took to her bed for a fortnight after the birth to recover – probably the only holiday she got, and the *fear an tí* had to cope with household duties as well as everything else. The way to restore herself to health was to get a pig badger (with the pink nose) and kill and butcher it. This was boiled with cabbage for several hours (can you imagine the smell?) and then served to the patient in the bed. After this, her health was restored and she got up and resumed her duties. I'd say you would too, after a feed like that.

People re-affirmed this story to us on the radio programme. Nobody who rang in, of course, ever ate badger themselves, or actually saw it being cooked. As usual, they had it on reliable authority from someone who had it from someone else – the normal unsatisfactory situation with fabulous stories like this.

However, two years ago I visited a primary school in Waterford city to take the pupils out on a field trip. Never was there so much rain. The field trip was impossible – time for plan B. I just happened to have a stuffed badger in the boot of the car, which I had borrowed from Dúchas for a different occasion, and was about to return it. I brought this in with me to show to sixth class. Two boys in the class were particularly animated at the sight of it and were dying to tell me what they knew about badgers. It turned out that they were Travellers and they told me, and the rest of the class, about being out one most exciting night with their uncles on the West Cork hills catching badgers. Why, I asked them, were they catching badgers? I was fixed with a pitying glance – what did I know? 'To eat of course,' was the answer. So now.

The badger isn't the only mammal to have unusual beliefs associated with it. The pine marten has too. This rare and elusive native Irish species lives in wooded habitats and never successfully made a transition to other habitat types when our woods were cut down. This is why it is so rare, the headquarters of its distribution being in County Clare and southeast Galway. It is a carnivore, killing for food. Its Irish name – *cat crainn* – indicates that it is an arboreal dweller, and indeed it was reputed once to have had squirrel on the menu.

Anyway, I wasn't long in the Biological Records Centre in the mid-1970s when I got a phone call from a man in County Sligo, who wanted to report a record of a pine marten. This pine marten had come into his shed and he had beaten it to death with his shovel. It was sufficiently unusual for him to go in and call his wife out to see it. And by the time he arrived back out with the wife to the shed where the dead pine marten lay, the nail in the tail was gone.

'What nail?' says I.

'What nail?' says he. 'Do yous know nothing up there in Dublin?'

Apparently pine martens have a six-inch iron nail stuck through their tails and this is why they are such ferocious killers. If you could get hold of this, you would have a powerful good-luck talisman. But they are very difficult to get hold of, as the pine marten reabsorbs it after it dies, unless you get it immediately. He had wasted time going in for the wife and by the time he got to examine the pine marten, the nail was gone – wouldn't you know! I accepted the record for my maps even though the animal no longer had a nail. It is, of course, illegal to kill pine martens now, under the Wildlife Act, and I've never heard from anyone who actually has a pine marten's nail in their possession.

Stoats are another mysterious lot. We don't have weasels in Ireland: they never got here after the Ice Age, although they did get to Britain. Our stoat has been isolated from its European relatives for so long, it is considered to be a separate subspecies. Stoats turn completely white in wintertime, in countries where snow lies on the ground for considerable periods of time, and this white fur is known as ermine. It obviously gives them an advantage in the snow, when creeping up on prey and, in turn, helps them to evade detection from predators such as foxes and large birds of prey. Such a winter coat would be a positive disadvantage to the Irish stoat, as periods when snow lies on the ground are so rare here, particularly on the east coast, as to be declared a national emergency when they do occur. Any stoat with a tendency to go white in winter would starve to death, or be quickly gobbled up, so the survival of the fittest has ensured brown coats only.

Legends have grown up about the stoat, not because of the colour of its coat, but because of its behaviour. It does not know its place – it is not afraid of humans. Stoats are very curious and will watch people going about their business, cutting hedges, saving hay and so on. Being watched by a wild animal unnerves people and makes them tend to ascribe human motives to animal behaviour, never an altogether sound idea. So we have stoats' funerals, stoats' parliaments – interpretations put on behaviour patterns which are not understood by the watchers. Now, we do have people ringing in to the programme who have seen these displays of groups of stoats with their own eyes, but what the explanation of them is, is not altogether clear. Not that that stops our listeners from declaring *ex cathedra*.

Ireland is one of the European strongholds of otters. These fish-eating carnivores are residents of our rivers and coasts. It is the same species that fishes the freshwater rivers and the sea. They are top carnivores, and, if conditions are right for them, all is fine in the levels of the food chain beneath them. As they are fish eaters, if there are otters in the rivers, there must be fish and enough food for the fish and enough dissolved oxygen in the water for all. So they are biological indicators of good water quality.

Otters dig burrows known as holts in the riverbank, which are entered underwater from the river. Here they sleep and breed. Holts are difficult to create, because they are burrowed right into the riverbank. Like digging a mine, there must be scaffolding in the shaft to prevent collapse. Otters use the roots of riverside trees as support for their holts, and they will only breed in an area where there are enough trees to provide this support. This, in turn, means that you only find otters in areas where there is a good environment.

Just how good Ireland is for otters was graphically brought home to me when I learnt the results of an otter survey carried out by the Vincent Wildlife Trust, a wildlife charity based in London. They employed two people – a husband and wife – to survey these islands in 1980–81 to ascertain the status of the otter. They divided the area into 10-kilometre squares and chose a representative sample (one in two) in each of the four countries to survey for otters. They looked in each square until they found evidence that otters lived there and then moved on to the next square. In England, they found evidence of otter in only 6 per cent of squares sampled. They found positive evidence in 20 per cent of Welsh squares, 73 per cent of Scottish squares and in Ireland they found positive evidence of otters in 92 per cent of the squares they surveyed. Twenty years or so on, we are still a stronghold of otters, a species which is now considered endangered in Europe.

I was amazed at the high turnout in Ireland and asked them how easy was it to see otters and how often did they encounter them. To my astonishment, they said that they had only seen otters once or twice, that all their records had come from otter spraints – otter droppings, in other words. These are very distinctive – tarry, with a

characteristic smell, containing fish bones – and are deposited by the otter in prominent positions as territorial markings. I looked at the researcher as she told me this, with her elegant blonde hair and her beautifully manicured varnished nails, and tried to picture her poking through droppings for fish bones or bending close to get the characteristic whiff. I must confess my mind boggled. I wondered what she told people at parties she did for a living?

We are obliged under European directives, as well as under our own Wildlife Act, to protect otters. How then are they coping with the recent establishment of mink in the wild? The mink is an American species that was bred in Ireland from the 1950s as a source of fur for the clothing trade. Although the first mink farms were established in 1950–53, it was not necessary to have a licence for such farms until 1965. Following the introduction of this requirement, the number of such farms declined, although the size of those remaining increased. More recently, the collapse of the fur trade has spelt the death knell for mink farms. However, mink have been escaping from such farms into the wild since 1961, when the first recorded escape occurred in Omagh in County Tyrone.

Mink in captivity are bred for their pelts, which are maintained by breeding as the pinky-brown colour so beloved of the fur trade. After a few generations in the wild, the colour reverts to the normal black colour, not desired at all by the fashion-conscious, so you can't even make a collar out of the one you catch marauding in the chicken house.

In the wild, the mink is a ferocious creature. There have been multiple escapes since 1961 and they are now established in all our major waterways. Not only do they eat fish but they also feed on freshwater crayfish, water birds and their eggs, frogs and rats. They are not averse to leaving the water altogether and visiting riverside farms to dine on chickens and ducks and they have even been known to eat rabbits. And, of course, they have no natural enemies here. None of their natural enemies in Canada were introduced here, nor indeed would we want any of them.

Because they have such a varied diet, they do not seem to have a negative effect on otter numbers. Their depredations are most keenly felt among water birds, which can be almost exterminated in an area heavily occupied by mink. Owners of fish farms and gamebird rearers (unnatural practices in themselves from nature's point of view – all those animals cooped up and fed with food brought in rather than produced in the area inhabited by them) can be particularly pestered by mink, who see the caged animals as a food source for themselves, and are very adept at getting hold of them.

All this is yet another example of the upset done to an existing order by the introduction of a non-native species without the normal checks and balances.

LICHENS – A MOST PECULIAR COUPLING

LIFE ON EARTH is believed to have begun three-and-a-half billion years ago – a mere billion years or so after planet earth was formed. This was apparently very primitive bacterial life and we can only deduce its presence from biochemical changes in the rocks where these bacteria once lived. They were able to exist for billions of years in the most arduous of conditions and, indeed, bacterial life is the most successful to this day. However, it was with the appearance of the chlorophyll molecule that life as we know it began to evolve. This chlorophyll could make sugar from the carbon dioxide and water vapour in the atmosphere using only sunlight as energy – photosynthesis – and with one mighty bound plant life began.

Initially this was primitive unicellular green algae in the sea, but over the millennia it emerged on to the land and diversified into other groups, such as the mosses, liverworts and ferns. But the algae had another trick up their sleeves as it were: they joined forces with another, non-green group, the fungi, and two became one – lichens.

And the lichen could boldly go where no plant could go before. This strange group is found everywhere we care to look. We are familiar with them on apple trees, roofs, gravestones and, of course, they provide the food for Santa's reindeer. They are so very successful because the whole is greater than the sum of its parts.

The algal part of the lichen contains chlorophyll and this is able to make food by photosynthesis. The fungal part is the distribution system – the railway tracks as it were. Fungal cells are rigid and this is what gives lichens their hard brittleness. The fungal colour often masks that of the algal component, so we get brilliant-coloured lichens – orange, red, purple, white and silver – as well as the duller black and olive green.

The whole structure only needs a surface to grow on. It has no roots, so it can grow on limestone rock, tree trunks, slates, frozen soil, whatever. It doesn't need to absorb water and minerals through roots, as is the case with higher plants. Lichens can also grow where it would be too poisonous for other plants. They can store heavy metal molecules in their cells, such as silver, chromium, cobalt – metals that would kill a more 'advanced' plant. In fact, it is sometimes possible to determine what metals are being released from a polluting source by analysing the lichens growing around the area. The cells in the lichens will contain enough evidence to blow the whistle on the polluter, but only if the pollution contains heavy metals.

So it is no wonder that they are hardy pioneers – the first to colonise an area. They are to be seen in all their splendour in Arctic regions where great stretches of tundra are covered in multicoloured sheets of lichens, which are grazed upon by the reindeer. They are an important source of food for them, particularly in winter, as lichens can live underneath the snow. They appear on volcanic islands as soon as the ground is cool enough to be colonised. They grow on dry sand dunes, where the crunch of them underfoot is one of the typical sensations felt when walking through this type of habitat.

Lichens are biological indicators *par excellence*. Their presence, or absence, on the tree trunks of an area depends very much on the quality of the air. While they may be able to accumulate heavy metals in their cells without harm, they are particularly sensitive to sulphur dioxide, a gaseous air pollutant. As they have no roots, they absorb all they need from the air and from the rain that falls through the atmosphere. If the air is pure and clean, lichens will grow in great abundance and variety. But if the air contains pollutants, particularly sulphur dioxide, the lichens will quickly absorb them and die. Sulphur dioxide gets into the air from burning fossil fuels such as coal and oil. So we might expect an absence of lichens in areas with lots of smoky chimneys and belching car exhausts, areas indeed where the air is not too good for our own lungs either.

But some lichens are more sensitive than others to sulphur dioxide. There are three forms of lichen growth. One form is like splotches of paint on a surface – just a crust of lichen firmly attached to the surface. There is just one surface area exposed to the air here, so crusty lichens can put up with a lot. Another form is a leafy type, joined by its edge to the surface it grows on, so that you can see the upper and the lower surface, which are often of different colours. These leafy lichens have more exposure to the air – two surfaces – so they get a double dose of any pollution going. The most sensitive form, the one which has the most surfaces exposed to the air, is the shrubby lichen. This looks like a hank of green steel wool hanging off a twig or on the bark of a tree. It has so many surfaces exposed to the atmosphere that any whiff of sulphur dioxide at all deters them.

So, if you want to know whether it is safe to breathe deeply out of doors in your area, go out and look at the trees nearby. All three types present, and you can hyperventilate if you want to – but, if the air is a bit iffy, you'll only find leafy and crusty ones. Crusty ones only and it might be no harm to wonder why this is the case. If you have no lichens at all growing on the trees in your area, then the air around you is too polluted with sulphur dioxide for them to get established.

I know where the black spots are, or at least I did, because in the 1980s I undertook a survey of the tree lichens of the coastline from Dundalk to Limerick. I had Leaving Cert students at the time up and down every tree, describing the lichens present and ticking them off on the list. Cork was the first area to be studied and the results gave a map with a classic pattern of lichen-type distribution. It was a series of concentric circles (more ellipses actually), with just crusty lichens occurring in the innermost area, the centre of Cork city itself. The next rings contained various leafy ones, and it was only when we passed the city boundary, that we encountered the shrubby lichens – the culchies as it were. But there were crusty lichens on the trees even in the centre of Cork and that was the case in all the big cities we encountered as we progressed year by year, from Cork to Limerick to Waterford, until, that is, we came to do the Dublin Survey in 1987.

Because the local authorities had monitors in the built-up city areas, it was possible to put a figure on the amount of sulphur dioxide each group of lichens could tolerate. So even when there were no monitors, we could say how bad the air was, judging by what lichens grew there. This work had been pioneered in Britain and they had figures over there too. When we compared results, it looked as if our Irish lichens were much more sensitive than the British ones, because ours could not put up with as much sulphur dioxide as the British ones could. Of course, suggestions were made by persons from across the water that we could not do it right, that the local authority monitors were inaccurate, that the lichen groups were identified inaccurately. It was with great pleasure that we showed them that Cork lichens were indeed more sensitive than the same species in, say, Newcastle. During the winter, it's much warmer and wetter in Cork than in Newcastle. Our lichens can grow and metabolise (and take in sulphur dioxide) all the year round. In Newcastle they close up shop in the winter (when levels of air pollution are highest) and sit it out unscathed in much higher levels than they could do in Cork. So there!

But what of Dublin, which we didn't get around to surveying until 1987? Air quality in Dublin in the 1980s had been the subject of much public interest. There had been a whole week of snow in January 1982 when we practically had a Minister for Snow (Michael O'Leary) to deal with the crisis. The cold air had sat like a lid over Dublin city and all the smoke from the countless chimneys had risen just till it encountered this cold inversion and filled all the space downwards from that. Never was there such smog. Although local authority monitors were all the while measuring the quality of the air on a continuous basis, the figures were not released until April of the next year. So it was possible to know the following April what air pollution there had been that winter, when it was too late to do anything about it. And, of course, the monitors were fixed in certain sites, so who knew what the air quality was like in areas away from monitors? Public interest grew, fanned by radio programmes such as Gay Byrne's morning programme, and it wasn't long till the figures for daily air quality were being read out on the airwaves during the winter months. There were indeed a few black spots around monitors in certain parts of Dublin but, of course not everywhere.

When we did our survey of lichens on trees in Dublin in 1987, we discovered that there were large areas in Dublin city where there were no lichens at all on the trees, not even the crusty ones. These

areas were not just around the monitors, which indicated black spots, but over all of the city centre and in stretches north and south of the Liffey as well. As in other years, we published the results. The following year, two things happened, completely coincidentally of course. An Foras Forbartha (where I had worked in the Records Centre for fourteen years) was abolished, and Mary Harney, junior Minister for the Environment at the time, brought in a law banning the sale of bituminous or smoky coal in Dublin. From then on, only smokeless coal could be *sold*, so that was what householders ended up using, although there was no actual ban on *burning* smoky coal.

Dublin's air was saved, but I was no longer in a position to monitor it. But if you look, there are lichens growing on trees where they definitely were not ten years ago, the awful smell of smog on frosty nights is gone. The respiratory health of the old and feeble is not at so great a risk, and fickle public interest has moved elsewhere. No longer are the figures from the monitors read out on a daily basis over the airwaves, proving the adage that the only news is bad news. Mind you, the trees round Trinity College were still bereft of lichens the last time I looked...

CHAPTER SIXTEEN

AGEISM –
INSECT LIFE CYCLES

AGEISM IS THE latest politically correct concept. Employers cannot advertise for young, energetic employees, even if that is what they want and the work patently needs young people to do it. So how come publishers of books on insects have been allowed to get away with rampant ageism for years, albeit the other way round? Look up a mayfly in any popular insect book. Go on, do. What you will get is a picture of the adult mayfly, notwithstanding the fact that it may only be in this form for one or two days out of a life cycle that lasts for a whole year at least. What does it look like the rest of the time? Why are we not shown? It is the same with butterflies or bluebottles or daddy-longlegs: it is the adult form that appears in the general insect books and you have to buy a specialised book to see what they look like in the earlier stages of their life cycle.

A butterfly, for example, may only spend a small proportion of its life as the familiar butterfly-shaped insect we all recognise, but will you find caterpillars or eggs in the general guide? The female butterfly lays eggs, sometimes up to one hundred, on the food plant that is right for that species, say the cabbage in your garden in the case of the common large white or cabbage butterfly. These eggs are like tiny sculpted pats of butter. They quickly hatch out into small yellow caterpillars with dark heads and the first thing they do is eat their vacated egg shell. They then proceed to demolish the leaf upon which they have hatched. Caterpillars are just eating machines, they are neither male nor female, they exist solely to eat. Gender is determined later when they pupate into butterflies.

Children are sometimes told that if they don't stop eating they'll burst, but has anyone ever seen a burst child? The worst that happens is that they get sick. Well, caterpillars do burst. They eat and eat and get fatter and fatter, a process some of us are all too familiar with. But caterpillars are built differently to humans. We have our hard parts on the inside and our soft parts on the outside and the more we eat the bigger our soft parts can grow. Caterpillars, however, have their soft parts inside a hard outer coat like a corset, which cannot expand. When the strain from the ever-increasing inside soft parts becomes too much, the outer hard coat bursts and falls off. The inner, soft coat can then harden on exposure to the outside air. And the caterpillar merrily continues eating, no doubt having moved to another leaf at this stage. Again it fattens up, again its girdle is killing it and again it bursts, no doubt to its great relief. Butterflies can burst four times in all, each stage of development being darker and hairier than the stage before.

The bigger and hairier the caterpillar gets, the more distasteful it becomes to the birds who have been tipping away at the original hundred that were laid by the parent butterfly. Small juicy caterpillars are much beloved of blue tits, who time the hatching of their young to coincide with the first big flush of caterpillars in the year.

So by the time the caterpillar gets to the hairy molly stage, it is one of ten rather than one of a hundred. Already it has changed shape and colour a few times – so you can see the difficulty for the book illustrator. It then leaves its leaf, climbs down off the plant, and crawls away to carry out the next stage of its life cycle, often over a footpath or a road, well away from the food plant where it has been gorging itself.

And it is at this stage that it is picked up by some curious passer-by and put in a matchbox and sent into the programme to be identified. And there we are, with this furry caterpillar found on a road with no food plant for a clue, half dead in a matchbox, and we are expected to identify it. The books only show the most exotic-looking caterpillars of the thirty-three butterfly species and over two thousand moth species we have here in Ireland. What to do? Well, if it is still alive because its packing was rigid enough, we can let it proceed to the next stage of its life cycle. Fortunately, it does not need any food for this. In fact, if it sees the food plant that it stuffed itself with ever again, it will be too soon. Whatever food it has taken on board has to sustain it now for the rest of its life. The eating part of its life is over. It has reached the end of the caterpillar stage and it must turn into a butterfly.

To do this it has to become a chrysalis first. It leaves the food plant and climbs up to a dry place. It is often found by curious humans, during its journey away from the food plant to a spot where it can form a chrysalis. I imagine this is because the caterpillar is no longer camouflaged against the food plant and its movement also attracts attention. However, it is now very furry and covered in distasteful hairs, so it is not attractive to birds, who couldn't fail to pounce on it if it was edible. So a hairy caterpillar moving purposefully and rapidly across open ground is definitely on the way to pupate. This can be on a twig, on a wall, under eaves; anywhere it can remain

unmolested for as long as it takes to become a butterfly. It then attaches itself and begins to spin a silken cocoon around its caterpillar body.

It *is* a silken case too, although in most cases the silken thread is much too fine to be of any interest to us. This is not so, in the case of the silkworms. Silkworms are the caterpillars of a particular moth that is of great commercial interest. This caterpillar feeds on the leaves of the mulberry tree, a tree that can grow in Ireland but is generally cultivated in warmer countries than ours. When it has finished eating and is ready to change into a moth, this caterpillar is of particular interest. It spins such strong silk that it can be collected and spun into the silk fabric that is so beloved of lingerie makers and haute couturiers. Silkworms were cultivated in central France and southern Spain until the 20th century, but it isn't worth the effort in these places any more. Farming silkworms is a very exact business. They do not like strong smells or sudden changes in temperature. If a loud noise occurs while they are spinning their cocoons, they will stop and turn their heads, thus cutting the silken thread. Once the silken cocoon is spun, the silkworms are taken away so that the silk can be unravelled and spun, because otherwise the silkworm, like any other caterpillar, would continue its metamorphosis into an adult.

Inside their cases of silk, all caterpillars change completely. The butterfly (or moth) stem cells contained in the caterpillar body begin to develop and grow. The caterpillar cells that it no longer needs melt down to provide fuel for the growth of these butterfly cells. And the butterfly is a completely different looking creature from the caterpillar that crawled up the wall. It is developing four wings, in many cases of a completely different colour to the caterpillar. It is growing antennae on its head, and six proper legs. But most interestingly of all, the butterfly will have no digestive organs. It may take the odd drink of nectar as it flies about, but its eating days are over. Its abdomen contains its reproductive equipment, because this is what this highly mobile, brightly coloured stage is for – sex and reproduction.

When all is properly formed inside and the time is ripe, it will burst open the cocoon case and emerge as a butterfly. The wings will open and be pumped full of liquid to make them rigid. The beautiful colours, carried on tiny little scales on the surface of the wings, will appear. The butterfly is now dressed for the ball, and that is what the rest of its life consists of – one long ball, where it displays and shows off to others of its own species in the hope of attracting a mate. And, as indeed in all of our cases in these matters, luck plays an enormous role. Butterflies cannot fly in the rain, and strong winds do not help their cause either, so they are dependent on calm, sunny weather to meet their true love. Birds are not averse to a tasty butterfly for lunch (they strip off the wings first before swallowing them). A giddy, excited butterfly in the first dizzy rapture of love can easily blunder into a strategically placed spider's web, where with one well-placed bite it is quickly dispatched by the ever-watching spider. If we had to face such difficulties, we'd never go outside the door.

But when all goes well, when the sun shines on a calm, hot day, there is nothing so evocative of summer as a group of colourful butterflies in the air over a meadow full of wild flowers. And, for the successful ones, the reward is great: mating is quickly followed by egg-laying on the food plant that sustained it as a caterpillar and then, spent, the butterfly expires. Mind you, if they didn't mate and remained virginal instead, they would still expire, because, since they don't feed as adults, they all run out of fuel in the end.

We see no butterflies in the winter, so what happens then? Well, the general situation is that they overwinter as a chrysalis. Once

they are safely in the cocoon, they can last like that for over six months. This doesn't help us to identify the creature sent in as a pupating caterpillar, as we will probably have lost the thing or be on a programme break by the time it hatches out. The brown hairstreak butterfly overwinters as an egg affixed to blackthorn twigs. The egg is laid next to the thorn on the twig and is quite unnoticeable. It stays there all winter, only hatching out the following year. The small tortoiseshell overwinters as an adult. It makes definite efforts to get into houses in the month of September, where it takes up residence in the hot press or, as was the case in our house when I was young, in the parlour curtains. When spring comes and the weather warms up and the sun shines, it sallies forth looking for action, one of the earliest butterflies to appear. Unless of course it was unfortunate enough to have picked our front room curtains to hibernate in. This was the 'good' room and we were never allowed in as children to mess it up. But at Christmas the room came into its own – the fire was lit, decorations were put up and the curtains were drawn. And the poor butterflies, who had never heard of Christmas, were kindly ushered out the window into the freezing cold, never to be seen again.

We do have several species of butterflies here who never heard of overwintering. These are the red admirals and the painted ladies, among others, summer migrants who arrive here by population expansion in July and August. Not that they fly here directly from Africa like the swallows and cuckoos. What happens is that, about the month of February, the adults lay eggs in the northern slopes of the Atlas Mountains in north Africa. The young hatch out, pupate, become butterflies fairly rapidly and then fly north across the Straits of Gibraltar in search of true love. They breed in southern Spain, their kids fly on to northern Spain, the next generation to France, and so on until, in the month of July, we receive the great-grandchildren of the first lot who bred in the Atlas Mountains in February. And, in

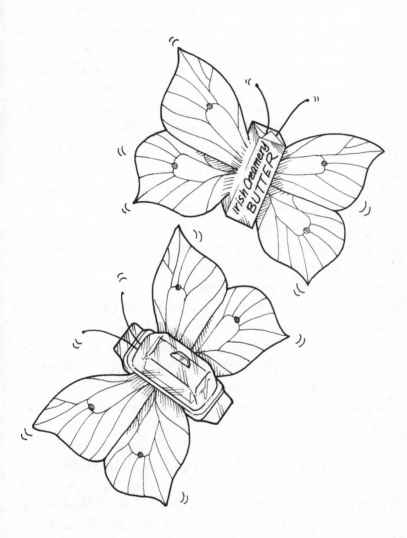

a good summer, the population expansion may continue right up to northern Scotland. But like many a summer visitor, they don't know when to go home. They have no inbuilt mechanism to instruct them to fly south when the days begin to shorten. You'd think they'd notice one sunny day in October that there's no-one around only themselves – no cabbage whites, no meadow browns and definitely no tortoise-shells – and wonder what's up. But they don't, and one awful night, around Hallowe'en, the first frost comes and that is the end of them until next July. So in fact red admirals are usually the last butterflies we see on the wing in the year. Only in countries further south where there is no winter frost do they survive, poised to start the whole population expansion thing again next year.

Did you ever wonder where the name butterfly came from? Well, there is a yellow butterfly, the brimstone, that flies in the month of May. The male is deep yellow and it flies long distances looking for the paler coloured females. This is a butterfly of limestone country, as buckthorn is its food plant. Good grass grows in limestone country, and, in the days when farming followed the seasons, cows out on the good grass produced enough milk for the churning season to begin. So it was that butter-making began in May, just at the time this large yellow, butter-coloured insect appeared, so what else could it be only the butterfly. The name subsequently spread to all such insects, regardless of their colour.

It is interesting that it is only in English that they are called after butter. They, along with moths, are Lepidoptera in Latin – which means scale-covered wings, féileachán in Irish, papillon in French, and mariposa in Spanish, none of which have anything to do with butter.

So the next time you see a picture of a butterfly in a book, remember that it looks like this for a very short period of its life. Much of the time it is in another state, of great interest to itself, if not to book publishers.

CHAPTER SEVENTEEN

RABBITS AND HARES AND THEIR UNSPEAKABLE HABITS

ZOOLOGISTS HAVE ALWAYS been interested in establishing which mammals are native to Ireland and which have been introduced and when. Looking at bones that have been unearthed from caves, they know, for example, that the woolly mammoth, brown bear, spotted hyena, wolf, Arctic fox, Irish giant deer, reindeer, mountain hare, Norwegian lemming and Greenland lemming roamed the country 35,000 years ago. Obviously, it was much colder then than it is now. Another Ice Age came after that, and when it finally ended 10,000 years ago, the Irish giant deer was gone. Not only did it not come back to Ireland with the disappearance of the ice, it was gone altogether – extinct – as was the woolly mammoth. Reindeer passed through, moving northwards, as the tundra in which they lived moved northwards with the warming up of the region. The tundra is also home today to the lemmings and

the Arctic fox. Bears and wolves re-established themselves here, as did the mountain hare, and they were joined by other species that moved up from further south with the deciduous woodlands.

So the mountain hare has had a very long history of being a native species: we can trace its presence back long before the arrival of man. It had the run of the country – no other hare species to compete with – and so it has made the whole country its habitat. It can live up in the mountains, as does its counterpart in Scotland. It also is equally at home in the flat lowlands, a habitat occupied by the brown hare across the water. It is a herbivore, which means it feeds on grasses, and, although hares have been recorded occasionally nesting underground, this is highly unusual – most hares live all their lives overground.

Its entire life is one of watchfulness. We were told as children that hares have no eyelashes and sleep with their eyes open, in a state of preparedness at all times to escape from danger – and boy is it able to run! To run like a hare is a common figure of speech: its turn of speed was obviously common knowledge. This is why it was considered a sport to hunt it, from the times of the Fianna to the present day. *Giorria* is the Irish name for the hare – a name that goes away back. I have sometimes wondered has this come from *gearr fhia* – short deer – in other words a substitute to hunt if deer was not available, a mini-version of the sport.

The hunting in the wild of a herbivore by a carnivore is a finely balanced affair. The carnivore has to estimate how much energy it will need to chase after the prey and what the chances of catching it are. Most of the hunting entails creeping up noiselessly, downwind of the unsuspecting prey and making a last-minute dash at great speed to catch it. In the wild, predators do not chase their prey for hours: the energy expended would not be worth it. If it is not caught in that sudden quick dash at the end, the predator cuts its losses and sneaks up on something else. So can hunting with a well-fed pack of hounds for a long period of time be said to be a natural practice? Can chasing a hare, an animal of open areas, in an enclosed course be fair and equitable, the so-called 'sport' of coursing? Why not call it what it is and stop trying to excuse it as part of what happens naturally in the wild – the hunter and the hunted. Hares would not have survived as long as they have if nature had stacked the survival odds so heavily against them.

We have other sayings that involve hares – as mad as a March hare being one. And, indeed, if you look at hares during the month of March, they do appear to be behaving in a completely deranged fashion. They seem to be having boxing matches with each other and then chasing around the field and sparring again. Of course, this is nothing more than courting behaviour and is no more mad in the eyes of the hare than our frenetic gyrating to ear-splitting 'music' is to us. Males spar and caffle with females, box and fight for real with other males and chase less lucky males around the field – much like many of our own social gatherings in a way! Females can have two or three litters a year with two or three in each litter, so it is a measure of how much predation there is on them from all sources that we are not overrun by them.

In the old days, people thought it was unlucky for a woman to meet a hare when she was pregnant, for she would then give birth to a child with a 'harelip' – a disfiguring deformity where the upper lip and sometimes the palate itself is cleft. This deformity occurs in one in 870 babies – in some cases there is an inheritance factor, in others it is purely random – but, of course, it has nothing to do with meeting a hare. Nowadays this condition is readily fixed by surgery.

Our hares do not turn white in the winter time as do the Scottish ones. They are both the same species *Lepus timidus*, but ours has been separated from the Scottish one for so long that any tendency it may once have had to do this has long since vanished. Thus we are considered to have a unique subspecies *Lepus timidus hibernicus*, found only in Ireland and distinguished from all others by staying brown in winter.

We do have another species of hare in Ireland – the brown hare. This hare is not native, but was introduced to Ireland during the second half of the 19th century. This is the lowland hare introduced to Great Britain, apparently by the Romans, and found in the flatter parts of that country (the higher ground being occupied by the mountain hare). Seemingly, it was introduced to Ireland for hunting, being fleeter of foot than the mountain hare. It never really got established here at all and has been recorded only in the north of the country, between Louth and Donegal. It is a different species to the native Irish hare but, in the field, the distinguishing feature is the black upper surface of its tail. Interestingly, it was the brown hare, as drawn by Percy Metcalfe, that was put on the threepenny bit when the Irish coinage was first minted in 1928. Like the hound on the sixpenny piece, it did not survive the change to decimal currency in the 1970s, still less the change to common euro currency in 2002.

Rabbits are not native to Ireland. They were introduced together with their name – *coinín* – by the Normans in the 12th century. The name *coinín* comes from the Latin *cuniculus* and, indeed, this animal is still known by that name in Denmark today. My brother, while working there during his time studying agriculture in college, was amazed to hear the continuous and unintelligible (to him) Danish being interrupted by a cry of *coinín, coinín*, as a rabbit bounded down the field. He hadn't been aware until then that they spoke Irish! The name travelled with the animal to America, and it is from the rabbit that Coney Island gets its name.

Rabbits were originally brought into Ireland as a source of food and became established in sand dune areas, where they could burrow easily. Such areas are often marked on old maps as warrens. Rabbits are very prolific and the term 'breeding like rabbits' has not crept into the vernacular by accident. Females can breed before they are a year old and can have up to seven litters a year, with about five babies in each litter. Rabbits rarely live longer than five years but, in that time, a female could have given birth to 150 young. No wonder they were eaten as food in olden times and, indeed, right up to the 1950s in Ireland.

Myxomatosis was the death knell really for rabbits as a general source of food. This is a viral disease that is carried by the rabbit flea and affects only rabbits. It was introduced to kill rabbits originally in Australia, where rabbits were causing terrible havoc, having been introduced by white people from Europe without any checks or predators. Myxomatosis was introduced to Ireland in the 1950s and decimated the rabbit population here. It is a particularly unpleasant disease for us to look at (and I am sure for the rabbits as well). The infected rabbit loses all sense of caution and wanders about in broad daylight with a horribly swollen head and practically blinded. People quickly lost all appetite for rabbit pie, in case they were eating early stages of myxomatosis that were not yet manifest. This disease only affects rabbits, not humans, but the public relations exercise was deadly. Rabbits have a certain immunity to the disease now, although it still flares up from time to time.

Foxes are great predators of rabbits and the huge decline in rabbits in the 1950s led to a decline in foxes too in certain parts of the country – proof of the ever-quoted dictum in textbooks that it is the prey who controls the predator, not vice versa.

Rabbits differ from hares in that they always live in burrows and rapidly scamper down them at the first sign of trouble. They communicate to each other by thumping their back legs off the ground and all grazing rabbits heed the warning and vanish – not much sport for hunting there. Links golfers hate them, as they burrow all over the golf course and the unwary golfer can easily twist an ankle in a burrow while in search of an errant ball.

Like hares, rabbits practise coprophagy. This interesting-sounding occupation means eating their own droppings. They feed on grass, which contains large amounts of cellulose, which is difficult to digest. Digestion takes place as the grass moves along the animal's intestine, but it reaches the end and is expelled before all the food value has been absorbed. So, in order not to waste good food, the rabbit eats these first droppings and runs them through again. Naturally each rabbit eats its *own* droppings – straight from the anus (there wouldn't want to be the slightest confusion about ownership!). The second time the call of nature comes, the rabbit emerges from its burrow and deposits the characteristically dried grass pellets around the entrance. There is not a calorie of food value left in them at this stage.

Rabbits are considered with a certain affection by people who do not have to accommodate them in the wild. The Easter bunny was originally a hare and the whole idea of chocolate Easter eggs being delivered by a rabbit is a complete travesty of the original fertility symbol that the egg at Easter is meant to represent. Or, considering the potential fertility of any given rabbit, maybe it's not.

OUR OWN
PERSONAL FAUNA

SOME YEARS AGO, I did a programme in the *Habitats* series with Derek Mooney on the human body as a habitat for wildlife – it was received with a mixture of fascination and horror. It was repeated on several occasions and now, in my *Creature Feature* series on Den TV, the one on the head lice is the one I'm asked most about. Where did I get the head lice? Do they really look like that? There was no question but that the audience were familiar with them: head lice have never gone away, even if other denizens of our bodies, such as fleas and bedbugs, are less commonly encountered, in our civilisation at any rate.

Head lice are insects that have evolved to live on the human scalp and nowhere else. They are flat and wingless and they hold on to hair with the claws they have at the ends of their six legs. They have a really tight grip, so that scratching or combing with an ordinary comb does not dislodge them. Washing does not drown them and soapy shampoos do not bother them at all. They live on human blood, which they suck from our scalps. They pierce the scalp with their specially modified mouth-parts and then suck up the blood into their bodies. Both males and females live in the hair and when they are big enough and the mood takes them, they mate. The female then lays fifty to a hundred eggs over a period of days, which she cements to the hair close to the scalp. These hatch out in seven days or so and continue the process. Each louse lives and feeds for up to several weeks so your head can be 'walking' after a few weeks if nothing is done.

Because they get all they need from a human head, they don't need to be able to see very well, so they have poor eyesight. They don't need to be able to fly, so they have no wings. They can walk, of course, and if a nice, clean habitat is within walking distance they will quickly walk from one head to another. They are adapted to a certain thickness of hair, so if they walk onto a head where the hair is coarse and thick, they cannot hold on properly and so do not become established. Our hair gets thicker as we get older, so adults are not as plagued with head lice as children are.

Adults, of course, sometimes get afflicted with a louse that lives in the hair, not on the head, but in areas further down on the body – *Phthirus pubis*, more familiarly known as the crabs. This louse only adheres to the much coarser body hair and is passed from body to body by close contact. Like the head louse it sucks blood and causes terrible itches as it does so.

There is a third type of louse that affects humans. This is a subspecies of the head louse – the body louse. It lives on clothing and only visits the body to feed. It thrives in conditions of poor hygiene where people have little chance to wash themselves or change their clothing. Like the other two lice, it causes terrible itches, but this one is even worse than that. It also carries disease, most notably typhus and relapsing fever. In wartime conditions or after

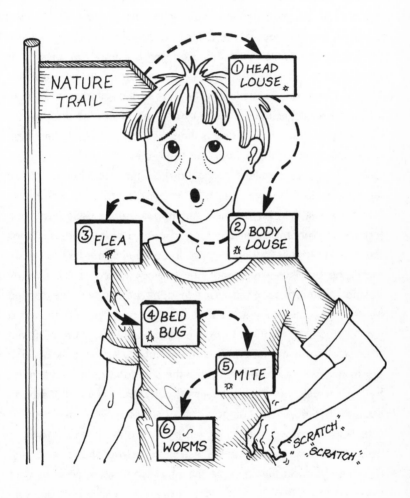

disasters, such as earthquakes and floods or during famine, much death is caused by lice-borne disease, often more so than by the disaster itself. During the Great Famine in Ireland in the 1840s, over a million people died, one-eighth of the population. Many of these died from epidemic typhus caused by bacteria-type organisms spread by body lice. The organisms are carried in the creature's faeces, which are deposited on the skin of the unfortunate human, who then scratches himself violently and introduces the disease into his blood stream. The patient suffers horribly from delirium, high fever and a rash and, without treatment, dies.

So maybe we shouldn't be so hard on the head louse, who at least doesn't carry fever. But how to get rid of it is the problem? Insecticides in the form of smelly shampoos are the usual treatment, together with horrible fine-combing to get rid of the bodies. But as this only kills adults, not eggs, it has to be administered twice – once to kill the adults present, and then a week later to kill the newly hatched-out creatures. People often don't bother with the second treatment because they feel so much better after the first and, as a result, two things happen. One, the hatched-out lot go on to rebuild a population in the hair and a month later your head is walking again and you're complaining that the shampoo didn't work. Two, by not carrying out the treatment properly and killing all the head lice with two doses of shampoo in the first place, you have allowed some that were nearly hatched out to survive the first dose and so go on to become resistant to the insecticide in your shampoo. So the next time you use the same treatment, it won't work because your particular population of head lice were already exposed to one sub-lethal dose and are now resistant to it. You have to try another brand of shampoo and insecticide.

The situation has now arisen whereby there are insecticide-resistant head lice doing the rounds. And head lice are always doing the rounds because they are not treated properly in the first place, with two doses a week apart. So if your children are head lice-free at the moment, try and keep them that way by making their hair unattractive to head lice. They don't like the smell of tea tree oil, although it smells fine to us. So a drop of that when rinsing washed hair ensures that they give your child's head the skip.

As well as our own special lice that attack us and no other species, we also have our own personal flea species – *Pulex irritans*, the human flea. Like many insects, this one has a whole life cycle of different stages and it is only the adult stage that bites us and sucks our blood. Fleas differ from lice in that they are compressed from side to side (as if they got squeezed in something) and they can leap. A human flea, which is about 3mm long, can leap 30cm, the equivalent of a 6-foot adult leaping 600ft.

So an adult flea leaps on us, bites us, sucks our blood and then is ready to lay eggs. Mind you, a female lays several lots of eggs (several hundred altogether), and needs a feed of blood before each laying session. The good news is that the small pearly eggs are not laid on our person but in furnishing materials, or mattresses, or blankets that happen to be nearby. They hatch within a week or two and produce worm-like larvae. These live by eating dust and skin cells and whatever else it finds on the surface it is on, and don't bother us at all. They thrive and grow big, bursting twice along the way, and after about three weeks are finished with this stage and are ready to move on to the next. They spin a silken cocoon and change to an adult inside. Now comes the clever bit: there is no point in coming out of the cocoon unless a nice juicy adult host is nearby to provide a meal, so they stay there, sometimes for months, until they feel passing vibrations. Then they quickly emerge, leap on the passing host, and dinner is assured. So stories of houses which have not been lived in for some time coming alive with fleas when people take up residence in them again are quite true.

While we have our own personal species, other species of flea are not averse to having a go at us. Cats and dogs have a species each, but both of these species will have a bite of us if we get too close to a flea-infested pet. Mind you, they would know after the meal of our blood that we were the wrong species (oops, sorry) but we still get an itchy lump all the same.

Our own flea is quite benign, really. It only wants a meal and leaves an itch, not like the rabbit flea, which carries myxomatosis, with fatal consequences, from one rabbit to another. The problem for us with fleas, really, is being bitten by the flea of another species, which carries a disease harmful to us. And the main culprit here is the rat. Plague is a rat disease, carried by the rat flea. It is in fact a fatal rat disease – so that's OK by us: the more that catch the plague and die the better. Alas, not so! When the rat dies, its fleas no longer have a living host and so they leave pretty sharpish. In olden times, when hygiene standards for waste and sewage in cities were non-existent, rats were an enormous problem. The pictures illustrating the story of the pied piper of Hamelin never show the piles of waste and filth on the streets that caused the rat problem in the first place. And inevitably, as happens in places of such squalor, some rat will have fleas with the plague and will pass it on to other rats. And, of course, some moidered and confused rat flea, whose host has died, will sample a taste of human blood if a handy human is nearby and start an epidemic of plague.

The bubonic plague in the Middle Ages in Europe killed 25 million people – one-third of the population of Europe at that time. It even got as far as Ireland, where people died of it in the 14th century – a punishment sent by God, it was felt, for wrongdoing. It was known as the Black Death because, when affected the buboes – as the lymph nodes were known then – swelled up and bled into the skin, resulting in black patches, death quickly followed. Bubonic plague is very rare in the world nowadays, but has not been completely eradicated in third-world countries.

An interesting aside on the Black Death is that we still carry the affects of it in our population 600 years later. Cystic fibrosis is a disease caused by a defective gene. This is what is known as a recessive gene, which means that, in order to have the condition, a person must inherit the defective gene from *both* parents. If a person only has one dose of the gene, they will be a carrier but will have no symptoms. This gene arises spontaneously by mutation in human populations. Statisticians can calculate the rate at which this mutation occurs and forecast how frequently it should be found. The figures hold true for Asian and African populations. However, among Caucasians, the incidence of this gene is much higher: one in twenty-five people are carriers. Geneticists tell us that a mutation that arises spontaneously (as this one does) would not be favoured unless it confers an advantage on the carrier. What possible advantage could the cystic fibrosis gene confer, when, especially until the 1930s, the disease was fatal and sufferers died in early childhood? It annoyed the scientists. They hate having their theories upset by the evidence. Eventually, in the last ten years they cracked it. It turns out that carriers of cystic fibrosis (and I suppose sufferers from it too, for all the good it did them in those days when their life expectancy was very short anyway) were immune to bubonic plague back then and the gene confers immunity to this day. When the plague hit Europe 600 years ago, a large proportion of those who survived did so because they had the cystic fibrosis gene and, as a result, even nowadays it occurs with above average frequency in Caucasian people.

If our own specialised lice and fleas were not enough to annoy us, we are also molested by a third specialised insect – the bedbug.

Again we have our own personal species – *Cimex lectularius*. Bedbugs belong to a family of blood-sucking bugs that parasitise birds and mammals. House martins and bats, for example, have their own personal species too. Our creature does not remain attached to man, but hides away among clothing during the day and comes out at night for a meal of blood. While its bite can be very annoying, the good news is that it has not been found to transmit any disease.

All these blood-sucking parasites of humans are much less common nowadays, thanks to the invention of synthetic insecticides – organochlorines and organophosphates. Imagine what it must have been like to live in Viking Dublin, say. All those combs that turn up in digs would have been used for removing lice from the hair. But, of course, they would remove the adults only. And a night on the tiles might bring home more personal livestock than you went out with. So the next time you see the chimps grooming each other, you know exactly what they are up to and why. It was probably a form of entertainment we indulged in ourselves in the days before electricity and DDT.

However, it is not only the insects that prey on us. When John Donne wrote 'No man is an island', he could have added the adjective 'uninhabited' and given his poem a whole new meaning! You'll be riveted to know that members of the arachnid, fluke and flatworm families beset us as well, although hopefully not all at the same time. Scabies is a most itchy skin infection caused by the mite *Sarcoptes scabiei*, which burrows into our skin and lays eggs. The burrows become inflamed and sore and itchy. The eggs hatch out into new mites, leave by the same burrows and infect the nearest person. A whole household can be infected very easily. The solution, nowadays, is to paint on an insecticide solution. God knows what they did long ago.

A veritable tribe of worms can live in our insides. Tapeworms and roundworms choose our intestines, while another group live in our lymphatic vessels. Threadworms are the most common roundworms we see in this part of the world. Their eggs live in soil and humans become infested from sucking fingers with dirty nails. Once in the body, the eggs reach the intestine and hatch out into white adult threadworms. And here they live quite happily, emerging only to lay eggs at night, causing a terrible itch in the lower regions of the back passage. Scratching and then sucking the fingers that have been used to scratch re-infects the patient, who is usually a child. Otherwise these worms cause no harm. It is patently untrue that eating sugar gives you worms: it does no such thing.

Dogs that have not been de-wormed can have a threadworm of their own, which behaves in the same way in the dog's intestine. However, if humans are unlucky enough to ingest this one, they may acquire a disease called toxocariasis. This may cause only a mild fever but, in severe cases, can cause pneumonia or, if a larva enters the eye, loss of vision. This is why it is vital to keep your dog wormed and to wash your hands and nails after playing with him.

The really dramatic worm that can infect our bodies belongs to the tapeworm family. These tapeworms can grow up to 9m long inside the intestine, having been acquired by eating undercooked infected beef or pork where the worm was encysted as a larva in the muscle of the animal. Amazingly, these enormous worms rarely cause any symptoms except the odd mild abdominal discomfort that could be caused by any number of reasons – a bad pint, the bag of chips you had on the way home, the box of chocolates you finished all by yourself. You'll be glad to know that such infestations very, very rarely occur here because we have proper meat inspection and adequate sanitary disposal of sewage – haven't we?

Worms can cause very exotic-sounding diseases in far-flung

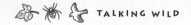

places. Guinea worm disease is caused by a worm ingested by drinking infected water. It makes its way to the skin after a year's incubation in the infected person. There it creates an inflamed blister that bursts, exposing the end of the worm, all poised to lay its eggs. The only way to get rid of it is to wind the worm gently from the skin using a small stick – no task for the faint-hearted, when you consider that the worm can be more than a metre long.

Hookworms are a nasty lot as well. They live in water and enter the body through the feet – washerwomen are particularly prone to them. They really know their way around the body. They burrow into the feet and enter the bloodstream. They then go to the lungs where they leave the bloodstream and get coughed up. Swallowing the sputum introduces them to the stomach and intestines. Here they live on the blood of the unfortunate host – enough of them can cause anaemia. Eggs are excreted by the human host, perhaps into water if unsanitary conditions prevail in the area, to hatch into larvae and wait for the next unsuspecting person to walk on them and let them in again. No wonder we are told not to drink the water in places where sanitary conditions are unknown!

Not that worms are the only thing you can acquire from infected water. There is another disease called bilharzia that occurs in most tropical countries and afflicts over 200 million people worldwide. This is caused by a creature that rejoices in the name of the fluke. Flukes have a particularly complicated life cycle, involving fresh-water snails, human bloodstreams (which they enter through the skin of someone wading or swimming in the infested fresh water), bladders and intestines (of the infected human) and the fresh water where the excreted eggs hatch out and enter another unwary snail. And the terrible thing is, there is no vaccine against the disease, which can progress in serious cases to liver cirrhosis and kidney failure. Fresh water in tropical countries should be treated with great caution and neither entered nor drunk lightly. Discretion is the better part of valour here.

Modern science has made great advances in the areas of sanitary disposal of sewage, thus making it possible to have clean water. At much less cost than armaments and war, these arrangements could prevail worldwide. Similarly, insecticides and other chemicals that kill the parasites mentioned above are quickly produced and administered if someone from the first world returns with more livestock on board than they went trekking or backpacking with – natives in those countries do not find such services made available to them. A lifetime of itch and misery from such unwanted human fauna is most often their lot. Napoleon (in *Animal Farm*) was right – some animals are more equal than others.

CHAPTER NINETEEN

WHAT'LL **IT DO** TO **YOU**?

I AM CONSTANTLY amazed, although goodness knows I should be used to it by now, at the attitude people have to creepy-crawlies, to those in particular that are unknown to them. Having come across a large black beetle, say, or a harmless aul' shield bug, they want to know what it is and what will it do to them? The arrogance of the second part of the question! As if creepy-crawlies sat around all day thinking of us and scheming for our demise. The truth of the matter is that very few things, either plant or animal in this country, do us any harm. We must live in the safest country in the world.

We have got rid of the wolf through constant persecution and trapping, although there is no scientific evidence that a non-rabid wolf ever harmed anyone in Ireland, and our present mammals are much more afraid of us – and with due cause – than we ever need be afraid of them. The occasional one that has a bad reputation such as 'the cornered rat' is actually put into that position by us. If we left it alone, it would quickly slink off. No mammal in Ireland will attack us (as, say, rhinos or elephants or lions or tigers or polar bears would). We only have one reptile – the viviparous lizard – no snakes, no alligators or crocodiles, no komodo dragon. We don't need to check our shoes before putting them on in the morning or make loud noises to warn unwanted visitors in the coal shed of our approach. The only danger in our rivers is the submerged super-market trolley or the odd bike.

We have no vultures circling overhead as their potential meal is in its death throes down below. (It took months of training and special effects to get the crows to appear so menacing in the film *The Birds* – they don't actually dive-bomb in real life at all.) Gulls and terns only dive-bomb us if we deliberately walk through their nesting colony during the breeding season, and they give us plenty of warning first. Swans have an undeserved reputation for being fierce, so much so that fine, hefty gardaí who wouldn't think a pin of wringing the necks of a turkey or two at Christmas, send for our swan expert Richard Collins if any grounded swans have to be dealt with. Yet male swans are only defending the wife and kids when they bristle up and hiss alarmingly, and we are well warned of their intentions. In fact, we have made aul' mollies out of some swans, feeding them bread and making them dependent on this. There was a court case in Dublin recently where a swan feeder claimed that she had been attacked by a swan. What probably happened was that the swan, who felt he had been short-changed in the sliced-pan department, chased the feeder who had run out of bread before he'd had enough, whereupon the fleeing feeder fell and broke a wrist. If children in buggies do not let go of the crust they are offering the swan, the bird, which can't actually see in close to its bill, simply grabs in the direction of the bread. This can sometimes appear as if the swan is biting the child's hand but it is not. These occasions can hardly be described as vicious attacks by savage swans. Frank Kelly's 'Twelve Days of Christmas' it is not.

Our fish are docile too. No flesh-eating piranhas shoal in our rivers. The waters are too cold (so far anyway) around our coasts for sharks to attack in these waters. The worst our largest shark can do to you is give you a heart attack when you see the size of him – 15m, as big as a double decker bus – swimming past you. But these basking sharks are vegetarian and only eat plankton. If you really are looking for thrills, you need to dive in warm waters with sharks, as I did once in the Red Sea with nurse and hammerhead sharks. That provided an adrenalin rush all right – for me at least, whatever about the sharks.

No, wild animals are guilt-free when it comes to unprovoked attacks on humans. Dogs, man's best friend, can be another matter, but I keep myself firmly out of the pet department.

When it comes to creatures that'll do things to you, we seem to be dealing with invertebrates – creepy-crawlies. Which of these actively seeks us out to attack us? Well, the main culprits seem to be Diptera – members of the fly family – and chief among these must be the mosquito. Yes, we do have mosquitoes in Ireland and always have had, long before global warming was ever heard of. We have up to twenty different species here. They lay their eggs in stagnant water and these hatch out into larvae that feed on small particles in the stagnant water. I grew them inadvertently one summer in my city back garden by not emptying the flowerpot containers of the rainfall that filled them on a continuous basis that whole summer. (They subsequently starred in the *Creature Feature* episode on mos-quitoes.) After a suitable length of time as a larva, they develop into fully mature adults with two wings and the long straggly legs and the whine (like a Mig fighter plane) that we are unfortunately so familiar with. The females need a feed of blood after mating before they can lay fertile eggs. The males are an altogether more likeable

lot, who feed entirely on nectar and plant juices. They do not even have the biting mouthpieces to draw blood.

But the females are well equipped in the biting department. They only fly at night and seem well able to detect where a vein is near the skin. They concentrate on ankles, wrists and faces, landing softly and piercing the skin, injecting anticoagulants into the wound, so that they can sip up enough blood before the blood clots. They can inflict a whole line of bites if they are allowed to work uninterrupted, so that you can wake up looking as if a sewing machine ran over your forehead or cheek.

The good news is that mosquitoes in Ireland no longer carry malaria or another disease known in the old days as the ague and have not done so in general since the 17th century. (Although there was a short-lived outbreak in Cork in the 1850s, caused by soldiers returning from the Crimean War.) The climate in Ireland was much warmer from the Middle Ages till the 1600s, and the malaria parasite was able to live and develop inside the mosquitoes here at that time. In fact, the last person of note to die of malaria in these islands was Oliver Cromwell, although whether he picked it up on his Irish campaign is not recorded. After his time, we entered a little Ice Age, as is most notably described by Charles Dickens who describes skating on the Thames, and the malaria parasite, though not the mosquito, was wiped out. The climate is warming up again, so I suppose there is always the chance that malaria will get back into our mosquito population again, particularly with the amount of foreign travel everyone seems to be doing.

Other members of the fly family that actively seek us out to bite are the midges. Anyone who ever worked on a bog is familiar with the midge, which emerges in swarms when the wind drops and bites our hairline and neck. There are actually two types of midges, both equally abundant I'm sorry to say. The Chironomids are non-biting midges, while the Ceratopogonids are the biting ones. The huge swarms dancing over the bog pools at dusk are really disco scenes where adult midges meet in order to mate. When the Chironomids have mated, the females go off to lay their eggs in the water, either on vegetation or in the water itself. The spent male meantime becomes food for a hungry fish, as indeed does the female when the eggs are laid. So would you begrudge them their few happy moments at the disco?

The Ceratopogonids are a different story altogether. Like mosquitoes, the females must have a feed of blood in order to be able to lay eggs, so this is their next task. Luckily, only a few of our more than one hundred species bite humans: the rest concentrate on birds, mammals or other insects. They don't actually bite their prey; they pierce their skin with their sharp mouthpiece and suck out the blood. Even though each midge is very small, no longer than 5mm, the bite is intensely irritating. This is because the midge injects its victim with a substance that prevents the blood from clotting so that it can extract enough to enable it to lay its eggs. It is this substance that causes us the pain and the itch and the lumps if we persist in scratching it. Once the female has secured her meal of blood, off she goes to lay her eggs in the water, where in summer the life cycle from egg to adult is only three weeks. No wonder there are so many of them!

In nature's scheme of things, both of these groups of insects are important consumers of detritus in water – in other words they are dustbin men. They are also a major food source for all carnivorous animals in fresh water. So maybe the fishing wouldn't be so good if our thoughts that they should all immediately become extinct materialised.

How do you keep them away from the back of your neck? There are all sorts of patented and expensive insect repellents that your pharmacist will happily sell to you. Others swear that smoking

cigarettes will keep them away. (Well, I suppose if you want to kill yourself to avoid being bitten, why not?) But a tried and true remedy that the old people used, and they were no fools, was a sprig of bog myrtle in your hat. Flies and midges of all sorts hate it and will keep well away from you.

The other nasty member of the fly family is the cleg or horsefly. This must be one of the most obnoxious of insects. Unlike many flies that are noisy in flight, this one flies in complete silence, selects a suitable expanse of skin, lands without us feeling it and then sinks its mouthparts into our flesh. The pain of the bite is the first indication we have of its presence. They are large, stout flies and make a right big bite, which can hurt and itch for ages afterwards. Clegs are not called horseflies for nothing – they inflict painful bites on horses and cattle too, driving them mad in the summer months.

And that's it. Most of the rest of the creatures that we think of as being 'out to get us' only attack us because they think we have attacked them first or we have got in their way. Bees and wasps do not set out to sting us. In fact, in the case of bees, this is the equivalent of *hara kiri*, as the sting gets stuck in our skin and tears away part of the bee's abdomen and she dies later. Bees are not suicide warriors – they only sting as a last resort.

Wasps don't die when they sting, but they don't do it for fun either. However, if you poke a wasps' nest with a stick, what do you expect? If you smell like a flower or you are eating sweet things in September or October, you mustn't be amazed if a hungry wasp comes to investigate a possible source of sugar. And if you flick her away, can you be surprised if she stings?

Jellyfish have stings in their tentacles to stun small creatures swimming beneath them, which can then be hoovered up into their mouths as food. The whole action is a passive one. Jellyfish may have a lot of power, but they don't know how to use it. So anything coming in contact with the tentacles will be stung, regardless of whether it is of any use as food for the jellyfish or not. The tentacles still sting when they are severed from the jellyfish, as sometimes happens with boat propellers, or when the jellyfish is washed up on the beach. If you touch them, you will get stung. They don't actively seek us out to sting us, any more than we actively seek out mice, rats, badgers and hedgehogs to kill as we drive along the roads.

THE **WATER POLICE**

WHAT IS CLEAN water? Is it water in which absolutely nothing grows, or is it water that supports a thriving population of fish, mayflies, damselflies, water shrimps and so on? The latter, you might be inclined to think, but you'd be on to your local authority in a flash if you turned on the tap and a nice wriggling stonefly larva came out and swam around in your glass. So our view of what 'clean' water is depends on what we want the water for.

Drinking water must be completely free of all creepy-crawlies, both visible and invisible, it must not smell and it must be crystal clear. In order to have it like this, all life must be filtered and poisoned out of it, and indeed enough residual treatment left in it so that nothing creeps into it on its journey from the water treatment plant to our kitchen tap. If you leave a glass jug of tap water on the table overnight, you can see the bubbles of chlorine sticking to the insides of the glass the next day. And if you doubt chlorine's efficacy as a water steriliser, try adding neat tap water to your prized tropical fish, or even your average goldfish. They won't thank you for it, even if they don't die on the spot. Water that has been left to stand or, at a pinch, is drawn from the tank in the attic, say through the cold tap in the bath, is much better for them.

Getting and maintaining water at this level of cleanliness is not easy (or cheap), yet all the water that comes into our houses is to this standard, even though most of it is used for flushing the loo, or washing clothes and dishes, or bathing and showering in. We actually consume only a very small quantity of this expensively cleaned water. We don't measure how much we use or pay as we go, so of course we are very *flaithiúlach* in our use of it. It would be a different story if we had to carry it back to the house in jars on our heads – then we'd appreciate the ease of turning on a tap.

In fact, all we do in our houses is turn clean water into dirty water and send it off again, hopefully to be cleaned by the local authorities before it becomes a source of pollution. And, indeed, this in the main, is what happens, or at least in the mains. The local authorities, with the help of some very useful wildlife indeed, clean dirty water before releasing it to rivers, lakes or the sea.

What are these useful wildlife? Bacteria, that's what they are – germs. These very primitive forms of life are able to break down all the organic waste that we put into our dirty water and turn it into carbon dioxide and water. All they need is plenty of oxygen to do the job, and this is supplied to them in the waste-water plants where our dirty water ends up. That is if you are on the mains in the first place. If you send all your waste-water to your septic tank, then you are depending on your own bacteria and the myriad of surfaces with air on them throughout the sand in the soak-away area, to do the trick – which it will, if you have not been conned by the advertising that urges you to kill all known germs dead. If you pour strong bleaches and other antibacterial products down the loo, how do you think your septic tank is going to work? Where are the bacteria that should be stuffing themselves in your soak-away pit? Dead, that's where they are, along with all the unknown germs. Your dirty water emerges still dirty at the other end, which may well be the groundwater that feeds your neighbour's well, or indeed your own well, or it may be the local river.

There is a very strict hierarchy of life in a river. Clean, unpolluted rivers will follow this exactly. All animal life needs oxygen to live and, in rivers, the oxygen available to the fauna is that which is dissolved in the water; so it is in short supply compared to the oxygen available to land-living animals. A clean river will have the full quota of oxygen in it and will support a full complement of animals. So we can tell by looking at the wildlife in a river whether it is healthy or not. Where do you find the creatures in a flowing river? Well, unless they have some strategy for staying in one place we'll find them all in a heap at the mouth of the river, washed down by the flowing current. This not being the case, what are the strategies?

One strategy is to swim very strongly and keep your place against the current. This is what fish do, but if you plunge into your local stream, pinkeen net in hand, you might be forgiven for thinking your river is in its death throes, for all the fish you find. Not surprisingly, an animal that depends on detecting flows and water currents to stay in its habitat is going to be immediately aware of clumsy, floundering you in the water and give you and your net a wide berth. A pity because, if you could definitely establish that there were fish in your stream, you could rest easy about the water quality. Fish are near the top of the food chain, so if they are present, then there is enough oxygen for them and the lesser creatures that they feed on. You could hang around quietly for a while and see if any fishermen in the form of herons or kingfishers appear. They wouldn't waste their time hanging around a polluted river, so seeing them about the river is nearly as good as seeing the fish with your own eyes.

But if you can't be quiet or patient, is there any quick way of establishing if the water is clean or not? Well, there is: you can look for creatures that employ the second strategy for life in a river, that is to hold on for dear life to any fixed surface in the water. If you pick up submerged stones or plants from the river and examine what you see, you can quickly tell, not only whether the water is clean or dirty, but exactly what state it is in.

There are some very sensitive souls clinging to stones or rocks. They need the full complement of dissolved oxygen to be able to thrive. These are the very well-known dragonflies, damselflies and mayflies. We are mainly familiar with them as adults flying in the air in their short mating period, but they can spend up to two years as nymphs in the water itself and they are easy to identify once you get the hang of it. Find these and the water quality is ace. Further down the class system that prevails in rivers, we have a group of less sensitive souls who need less oxygen to survive and will be found in somewhat iffy water. Caddis flies and stoneflies are in this category.

What makes rivers polluted in the first place? In great industrial countries like Germany, rivers, such as the Rhine and the Ruhr, are polluted by chemicals from their industrial zones. These poison the rivers by directly killing the life in them. So if you go boating on the Rhine, the water will look perfectly clear, there will be no obnoxious smell, but the river is dead, poisoned. Only now, in the 21st century, are they getting round to making life tolerable for the fish. Something to keep in mind the next time we hear some German tourist giving out about environmental conditions in Ireland.

On the other hand, we pollute our rivers here by putting in too much organic material – sewage and animal slurries in other words. This is perfectly good food for the decomposers in the food chain and they set to with gusto availing of this free food. However, they need oxygen to carry out this decomposing work and, in the order of things, they are able to lay first claim to the dissolved oxygen in the water and to hell with the fish and the mayflies and the dragonflies. The oxygen grabbers par excellence are the bacteria and, if levels of organic pollution are high enough, the bacteria will reign supreme, with no dissolved oxygen for anything else.

If the pollution levels are not so high, the invertebrate decomposers get a chance. In somewhat polluted waters, we will find lots of water lice and water shrimps working away on the food source and reproducing in big numbers. We will also find leeches, lots of them. These are only a pale imitation of the ones that had their fifteen minutes of fame in the picture starring Katherine Hepburn, *The African Queen*. Those ones were as long and as thick as a little finger and required massive amounts of blood to keep them going. Our leeches are tiny thin things, interested in snails and passing fish. They can't bite us or suck our blood – their jaws are not remotely in that league.

Interestingly, the big African leeches are now proving very useful from a medical point of view. As they need to suck blood for a long time from the small wound they have made in their host, it is of great importance to them that the blood they are imbibing doesn't scab over or clot before they have had enough. Accordingly, they inject an anti-clotting agent into the wound to keep the blood flowing freely. They are now being used in anti-clotting treatments for people who are prone to blood clots, either in their entirety (the entirety of the leeches, that is!), or if that is too off-putting, extracts from their chopped up bodies are used. It doesn't do to be too squeamish.

If the water is so full of organic matter that it is entirely the domain of the bacteria, that doesn't mean that there are no invertebrates there at all. Bloodworms, red wriggly creatures, have a form of haemoglobin in their blood, like we do ourselves, and this is able to store oxygen and keep the bloodworm going. And finally there is the charmingly named rat-tailed maggot. This creature sticks a part of its body up into the air and breathes through that as though it were a snorkel. It is thus independent of water conditions.

So in a perfect river we would expect the whole range from the mayflies right down to the rat-tailed maggots. There should be some of the good, the bad and the ugly there. But if we find, on a cursory examination of half a dozen stones, that the top end of the quality scale of creatures is missing, then we need no lab tests or elaborate water analyses to tell us that something is depriving the sensitive dwellers of their essential oxygen – and no prizes for guessing what it is.

The Water Pollution Act allows for water polluters to be fined heavily and it is fairly easy to find a source of pollution, downstream of which water quality deteriorates drastically, and fine accordingly. But that's not the only way rivers get polluted. As mentioned before, Irish lakes and rivers are polluted by fertilisers and slurries, which, when in the water, not only increase the growth of the oxygen-loving bacteria, but have another string to their bow, as it were. Farmers and gardeners know very well that they can get more plants to grow, quicker and stronger, by applying fertiliser to the soil where they grow. Well, it's the same with rivers and indeed lakes: if we apply fertiliser to them, the plants there will grow with great enthusiasm. So fertilisers sprayed on fields just before rain may well be washed into local water bodies, as may much of the slurry that is spread on farmland. The phosphate, in particular, in these slurries is like Christmas and their birthdays together to the green algae in the water and they grow and grow until the whole thing can turn into green algal soup.

So what? You might say – aren't these fellows plants, with the magic chlorophyll aboard, able to photosynthesise and fix carbon dioxide and give off oxygen? Surely they are adding to the oxygen in the water? Yes, but – there's always a but – they only do it during daylight when there is sunlight to give them energy. At night, like every other living creature, they need oxygen to keep going and, with the bacteria, they are first in line for any that's going. (The removal of flowers from sick rooms at night is not just because of an old wives' tale, although you'd probably want to have the Botanic Gardens in your room before it would be a matter of life and death.) Just before dawn, oxygen levels are at their lowest in water bodies. Not much point saying to the fish and the mayflies, hang in there for an hour or two and you'll be grand. And as more and more phosphates enter our water bodies (from our own profligate use of phosphate-containing washing powders as well as everything else), the number of rivers and lakes of pristine quality gets smaller every year. But we, of course, have to wait until there's nothing left but rat-tailed maggots and bloodworms everywhere before we take action.

Is there nothing in nature that will clean our water bodies? Well there is, actually: they are called zebra mussels, and they just love green algae. Once in a water body full of green algae they grow rapidly, eating the algae and cleaning the water. But these are foreign invaders. They came here originally on the bottoms of fresh-water boats from the Caspian Sea, and are completely out of balance with our ecosystems. They grow like the clappers and block up water pipes, foul ropes and boats and generally cause more problems than they solve. They don't eat themselves out of house and home, because there is no shortage of phosphates being washed into our rivers and lakes, and so no shortage of green algae for them to eat. Now, if only we could invent something to feed on *them*!

GALLING INFORMATION

WHAT DO ROBIN'S pincushions and oak apples have in common? Well, they are two of the more dramatic galls that we find on plants. Robin's pincushions are bright pink spherical tangles on the leaves of wild rose, and oak apples are the wrong name for the brown spherical marble gall that grows on oak. (The gall that is correctly called an oak apple is another type – a pinkish spongy spherical mass that also grows on oak.) These galls are really cancerous lumps grown by the trees in response to an outside stimulus and the outside stimulus is caused by an insect, the gall wasp. The gall is where the insect has been living and, by autumn, it is empty, with an exit hole marking the escape route of the mature gall wasp.

This wasp is completely different from the black-and-yellow one that we are so familiar with, particularly in the month of September. That one is a social wasp – it lives in a nest together with thousands of other wasps and works in harmony with others to rear young. The gall wasps, on the other hand, are solitary creatures; they have no nest or hive, but they do have a most peculiar and complicated life cycle. There are many different types of gall – artichoke gall, spangle gall, knopper gall, spiked-pea gall, silk-button gall – and they are all caused by a particular species of gall wasp that has a fully dependent relationship with the host tree.

Oak trees are particularly favoured by gall wasps, as about 86 per cent of all gall-making species of wasps form galls on oak. All the above-mentioned, with the exception of the robin's pincushion and the spiked pea, are oak galls, and you can often get several types on the one tree at the same time. The business starts in spring when a wingless female gall wasp emerges from the soil and climbs up the trunk of the tree and lays eggs at the base of the buds. These eggs hatch into larvae that, by their presence in the buds, cause the plant tissues to stop their normal method of growing and grow into a gall instead. This is just what the larvae want, because it is these galls that are their only food source.

So the galls provide abundant food for the herbivorous larvae, who feed away for many weeks. They then pupate and emerge as winged adult wasps, both male and female, which have, by a natural segregation, developed in separate galls. These then mate in the usual way and the female goes off to lay eggs.

But this is quite a different female from the wingless affair that climbed up the tree in spring to lay eggs, and this is where this whole group is so weird. This winged female is a fully mature female, it has mated with a fully mature male and it is going to lay its eggs, not back on the buds of the oak tree from whence it came (that would be too ordinary altogether), but somewhere else. In the case of the marble gall wasp, it lays on a Turkey oak, and in the case of the oak-apple gall, on the underground roots of the oak tree. And these eggs hatch and stimulate the growth of new galls where they were laid. Inside, the larva munches away, and eventually they all mature as one thing only – wingless females. Now, these wingless females are asexual. They are able to lay eggs without any mating – eggs that go on to become either fully sexual males or females.

This whole procedure is called alternation of generations, where a sexual generation is followed by an asexual generation. Each generation forms its own type of gall, either on different parts of the same tree or on different species. As every stage of all these species is quite tiny, you can imagine the research and dedication that went in to finding this out.

An interesting thing is that the Turkey oak, an evergreen, non-native species here, is the other half of the life cycle in the case of both marble galls and knopper galls (those cauliflower-shaped galls on acorns, which render them useless as seeds). Both trees must be present before the life cycle can occur. There must have been a long time in Ireland when we had neither of them, because we had no evergreen Turkey oaks for them to complete the life cycle on. We could only have had the oak-apple gall, which used the buds and the roots of the same native oak species, turn and turn about.

Marble galls, believe it or not, were actually introduced into south-western England about 1830, because the galls can be used for making ink and dyes. The gall wasp species subsequently came here and, of course, by this time we had Turkey oak in the estates of the landed gentry. The knopper gall seems to be a more recent affair, as we frequently get samples of acorns with this gall sent in to the programme by people who are completely mystified as to what it might be. It would seem that a way of getting rid of it is to have only one species of oak in the area, as the wasp needs the two species of trees in the same area to complete the life cycle.

Sycamore, willow, wild rose, all have their own galls too. Often the gall is not just food for the host gall larva, but many other

species muscle in on the free source of food. In fact, if you were to gather, say, a robin's pincushion gall at the end of winter and keep it in a glass jar, you could find that as many as seven different species of insects would emerge in due course. True communism!

Wasps aren't the only group that causes galls to form on plants, but they are by far the most common. A particular species of sawfly (not the timber-eating, terrifying-looking horntail) gives rise to the red bean gall on willow. Gall midges attack lime trees, causing bright red galls to form at the bottom of leaves, which then become stunted and hairy. Aphids get in on the act too, and there is a particular species that causes galls on the midribs of the Lombardy poplar. But, in general, none of these galls does any great damage to the trees. They all attack deciduous trees so, in many cases, the galls are on leaves which fall in autumn and the tree starts with a clean slate, as it were, the following spring. In any event, unless there was a ferocious number of galls altogether, there will be enough healthy leaves to carry on the growth of the tree.

It is when the gall grows on the reproductive part of the tree, as in the knopper gall on the oak tree, that danger arises. Acorns like this will not germinate and, in some cases, every acorn on the tree is so affected. Enough years of this happening and the reproductive capacity of the tree is compromised. The solution is to remove the Turkey oaks, the non-natives, although these can be fine, well-developed, beautiful trees too. Decisions, decisions.

CHAPTER TWENTY TWO

AN **DÚLRA BLASTA** – EDIBLE **WILDLIFE**

THERE IS A GENRE of television – and indeed radio – programmes where people are cast adrift, as it were, into the environment and told to fend for themselves, living off nature, with none of the inventions of the modern age. They are to become hunter–gatherers for a week or a fortnight, and our entertainment is seeing what kind of a fist they make of it. It is 5,000 years since people lived in Ireland as hunter–gatherers, and there have been such phenomenal changes to the landscape in the intervening millennia, that Mesolithic man would be hard-pressed to recognise the place, never mind live here for a fortnight.

Farming has been devoted to ridding the environment of 'useless' wildlife and replacing it with carefully selected, high food-yielding plants and animals. Eighty-five per cent of our land belongs to the farmers, so there are really very few places for wildlife, edible or otherwise to live. Notwithstanding this, I made a series of six television programmes for TG4 called *An Dúlra Blasta* – the tasty

environment. In this series, a guest and I visited an area and prepared a meal, the main ingredients of which came from the wild. It wasn't a survival programme or anything like that – it was just a way of drawing attention to the many wild things we still have that are edible.

The seashore was a magnet to our Mesolithic forebears and, not surprisingly, we based three of the six programmes there. The easiest things to find were the shellfish that clung to the rocks – that is, if you had found a suitable rocky shore in the first place. It couldn't be too exposed, or the shellfish would be dashed off the rocks, and it had to be free from any possible threat of sewage, as shellfish are, in the main, filter feeders and take in whatever is in the water.

There are lots of shellfish that cling to rocks, some much more desirable than others. Mussels are top of the league, followed by periwinkles. Limpets are edible too, but only the inner half of the animal. The kitchen midden on Omey Island, which is 5,000 years old, held shells of these same species. A midden is Mesolithic man's rubbish dump, and it was interesting to compare the size of the periwinkle shells found there with modern periwinkle shells – they were much bigger then. The midden also included oyster shells, obviously long since eradicated by gathering from the lower shore where they could be found at low tide. They occur now in deeper waters, or more likely in oyster farms.

There is a shellfish called a topshell, which looks like a rounded periwinkle, but it causes vomiting, so we left it alone. Of course, there were more of these than of any of the others, so obviously we weren't the only ones to know this. The rock pools, when the tide was out, yielded food too. Several sorts of seaweed can be eaten – *duileasc* (called 'dulse' in English) and carrageen moss – but most of the seaweeds could not: they were thick, coarse things. There were small, little prawns and shrimps running round the pools and little crabs, but they were easier to see than to catch. All in all, you'd be hard pressed to gather enough food for a family in the time between the tides when the lower, food-bearing part of the shore was exposed.

A muddy shore at the head of an estuary also proved to be a source of food. Many species of shellfish bury themselves in the mud when the tide is out, so by looking for telltale holes in the muddy sand and acting swiftly to dig out the occupants, we were able to get cockles, razor shells and gapers. Again, a lot of hard work for quite rubbery food.

Did prehistoric man ever eat any vegetables? Well, actually, many of our garden vegetables were originally seashore plants which, by careful plant breeding over the millennia, have turned into the mild-tasting vegetables we now enjoy. Their wild forebears were a rougher, tougher bunch. Sea rocket grows on the strandline and is hot and peppery to the power of ten. Sea kale and sea beet are both sandy shore plants (not that we gathered sea kale – it is now so rare as to be protected under the Wildlife Act). Sea beet is the same species as sugar beet and should be the real reason why we object to the genetic modification of sugar beet. As you will remember, there were trials of sugar beet, which had been genetically altered so as to be immune to weedkiller. Fields planted with the genetically modified crop could be sprayed with weedkiller as the beet grew, thus reducing competition with the weeds and producing a better crop. Now, the sugar we get from sugar beet is a chemical – $C^6H^{12}O^6$. There are no plant cells or chromosomes, altered or otherwise, in our sugar bowls. So in this case, it makes no difference to us if the plant is genetically altered (as opposed to genetically modified maize or soya, where we actually eat the plant cells). So what good reason could there be to objecting to it?

Well, genetic modification means that the change is carried from one generation to the next, so the sugar beet's pollen would have the changed formula. If this modified beet grew near the sea, its pollen could fertilise sea beet, its wild forebear, and the genetic modifications would enter the wild plant. And then we would have super weeds, immune to weedkiller, and the modification would have escaped from a controlled situation into the wild. And that, in my book, is bad.

For one programme, we made a quiche with the sea beet in it and it wasn't too bad at all. We also collected glasswort – small individual plants that grow in the mud near the water's edge which are supposed to taste like asparagus. In a pig's eye it does – it tasted like boiled string.

Collecting bigger food that might provide you with a decent bite required equipment. Crabs, lobsters, shoals of mackerel, all come into shallow waters but, unless we had a boat and fishing lines or lobster pots and all day and half the night, these things were not attainable. As it happened, TG4's budget rose to these things and we feasted sumptuously, but if you were poor and starving and only walking along the seashore, with no fishing equipment – tough.

It was much more difficult to find food away from the seashore. We needed woodlands, or at least decent hedgerows, and it had to be autumn. Naturally we contrived this for the programme and collected blackberries, sloes, haws, crab apples, rowanberries and elder-berries. But with the exception of the blackberries, you'd be in a poor way without sugar. No wonder beekeeping was such an important occupation of the monks in Christian times. Mesolithic man hadn't the luxury of a sweet tooth. Woodlands in autumn are also full of mushrooms and, with experts advising us every step of the way, we cooked a most exotic-looking mushroom stew. DO NOT TRY THIS AT HOME! There are several mushrooms in this country that can kill you stone dead and, unless you know what you are at, desist.

This abundance of food is good for animals too, so we could have had a juicy pigeon or rook fresh from the stubble fields. Deer and hares are also well nourished at this time of year, but we contented ourselves with a rabbit (not, of course, a contemporary of our hunter–gatherer forebears, but introduced a mere thousand years ago by the Danes), washed down with elderberry wine that we had, in the tradition of televised cookery programmes, 'made earlier'.

The whole experience was a salutary one and it certainly stopped me for a while making disparaging remarks about farming and gardening practices. Hunter–gatherer is a full time occupation and you could see how the diet could be boring and monotonous, with periods of shortage and scarcity. Interesting to think that all wildlife, with the exception of us, are in fact hunter–gatherers. No wonder they congregate when a large supply of food is found! How are they supposed to know that it is your field of wheat, or your goldfish pond?

YOUR **HOME** AS A **WILDLIFE HABITAT**

YOU SHOULD NOT be at all surprised to realise that you share your home with an abundance of other wildlife. The really surprising thing would be if you had actually succeeded in keeping everything out – you would have to be living in a sterile bubble. The thing is, how much can you tolerate? Can you live and let live? Would you rather not know what shares your house with you? Does it really matter, anyway? Will it affect your physical health or just your nerves?

Well, the creatures that share our homes vary from the visible and obvious to things you'd never know were there. Mammals, I suppose, are in the first category. Whoever coined the phrase 'as quiet as a mouse' must never have lain awake in the dead of night listening to the racket made by mice scurrying across wooden spaces – between the ceiling and the floor above or behind the wainscoting. Or never heard the nibbling and rustling as it mooches behind the sideboard or the wardrobe or the chest of drawers. Field mice and house mice are both guilty of such behaviour and their numbers and nightly shenanigans increase as the weather gets cold for winter. Someone recently sent me what they described as a hibernating mouse. You wish! It was as dead as a doornail because, of course, mice don't hibernate and this one was dead and not sleeping. Ultrasonic sound seems to be the latest way of convincing them to leave your house. I've seen it work myself and equally I have heard perfectly true complaints that the mice gather and dance around the plug – perhaps those were deaf (as opposed to blind) mice. There's a lot to be said for the old food chain. A cat or terrier with proper instincts should keep the house free from such unwelcome visitors.

Bats seem to terrorise some people who have them as summer residents in their attic. A dose of positive thinking is needed here. These animals are carnivores that come out at night and eat nocturnal flying insects – so think, no more biting midges or mosquitoes, no more daddy-longlegs or big, hairy moths flying in the window when you open it to get a bit of air on a sultry August night – and no, the bats won't fly into the room. Only very inexperienced ones do that and they will fly out again if you put off the light and leave them be. Anyway, you might as well make a virtue out of necessity, because all our bat species are protected under the Wildlife Act and you'd be a criminal if you damaged them or interfered with their habitat while they were there, even if you think it is *your* roof space.

Mind you, people have complained to us of having other mammals living in their homes. One woman who owned a shop had a grey squirrel in residence in the attic. It used to descend after hours and eat the chocolate bars, leaving papers around the place and reducing the profits. She didn't want to wall it up in the attic and she could never nab it in the shop. Short of cleaning out the shop and leaving only one bar in a live cage trap (so that it could be released far away from the sweet shop), I couldn't think of anything else to do. I did suggest it might draw curious wildlife-lovers to the shop, but she wanted less attention rather than more!

And then there was the other couple, who were doing up an old house in County Clare and encountered a pine marten living in the roof space. Now, this was a big animal, with lots of droppings and smells, and they didn't really want to share with him. Pine martens are so rare that the local wildlife ranger was happy to come to the rescue and take the animal to another part of Clare, from whence it could not home back to its attic.

Foxes occasionally come indoors and, again, if startled, can get themselves into places from where they can withstand a siege – under floorboards, in attics. One such fox starred on *The Joe Duffy Show*, for weeks as it seemed. So mammals show no mercy, and you only have yourself to blame if you get behind with the house repairs.

But some stowaways in the house do not wait for holes and cracks to appear to get in. Your latest bargain at the auction house may already have residents *in situ*, who are only delighted to spread to unoccupied furniture once safely installed in the parlour. I speak, of course, of woodworm who are not actually worms at all, but beetles – the common furniture beetle to give them their full title. People are perfectly right when they say that woodworm do not attack highly polished good furniture. They cannot lay eggs on this. What the adult beetle is looking for is rough, unplaned wood such as you get on the cheap plywood backs of furniture or as drawer bottoms. The eggs can adhere here and when the larvae hatch out a month later, they burrow straight down into the timber. Again, the rule about fine furniture made from polished hardwood obtains. The larvae can only eat sapwood, which they do with a vengeance, making tunnels in the softer parts of your furniture for up to three years, safely inside, hidden from your eyes. After this time, it forms a chamber near the surface – amazing how it knows where the surface is – and pupates. The adult beetle cuts its way up and flies up to the ceiling leaving behind the characteristic woodworm hole and a trail of sawdust. So by the time you see the hole, the deed is done, and the adults are having a merry fling on the ceiling, before starting the same procedure all over again. Now they have the run of your house and can infest your wooden floor or any pine furniture they may find. They don't like really dry houses so keeping the place warm and dry is one way round them.

Of course, if you have a stately ancestral home, you won't be worried about mere woodworm. You'll have an altogether better class of pest – the deathwatch beetle. These beetles only infest damp hardwood, so if you've lost a few slates off the oak roof beams, you are a likely candidate. These are the original head-bangers. It can be quite difficult up there in the dark, trying to attract a mate, and after the ten long years you have spent as a larva, eating tunnels in the timber, you are quite desperate. So what the sexually mature, adult deathwatch beetle does (and the female is just as brazen as the male in this respect) is to attract attention by banging its head against the timber on which it stands. This brings them running and the cycle can begin again. The story goes that if this beetle is heard in the house, someone is going to die. You'd have to be very quiet in the stillness of the night to hear these sounds, particularly in a big, old house – which you would be if you were up keeping watch over someone very ill. But why spoil a good story with the facts?

Bedrooms are good places for creatures who live in fabrics, such as wool blankets, feather pillows and carpets. Chief among this tribe are the clothes moths. People used to live in fear and dread of them and every October you'd be asphyxiated in church by the mothball smell off the winter coats and jackets that had just had their first outing in six months. Mothballs contain naphthalene, which deters female moths from laying eggs in garments that reek of it. And, of course, it's only the caterpillars that do the eating – the brown clothes moth that we sometimes see flying out of a rarely opened wardrobe doesn't eat any more.

There are different species of clothes moths, but one that inspires a particularly awful fascination is the case-bearing clothes moth. No, this does not come with a suitcase in which to pack the clothes it wants to eat; what it does is worse than that. The larva, when it hatches out from the egg, begins to make a case or cocoon around itself from pieces of the fabric it finds itself in and nibbles away at this. As it grows, it makes its case bigger and bigger. Of course, it is the same colour and texture as the carpet it is destroying, and it is only noticed when extensive spring-cleaning or the like is being carried out. Carpet beetles can also reside in the carpet and they can make a fine old job of it as well. They have voracious cigar-shaped larvae with a tuft of hair at the rear end.

All of these diners on fabrics originated in the nests of birds and rodents and lived on feathers and rodent fur. They have much more abundant food in an Aran jumper or a stored blanket than they ever got off a mangy rat. However, modern-day fabrics are too much for them. They cannot eat the man-made fibres that come from oil, such as nylon, polyester and dralon and so, as we move more and more to these fabrics, particularly in our soft furnishings, times are becoming tough for the clothes moth. Soon we won't understand the expression 'that's been mothballed for years' – or worse, think it means something else altogether.

Another creature that can make its presence felt in our homes, although we may never actually lay eyes on it, is the mite. There are several species of these and they are at maximum about a millimetre long, about the size of a full stop. The dust mite lives in large numbers in the dust of mattresses and carpets. It grows by shedding its skin, which it leaves carelessly lying around. This is even smaller than the mite itself and can be inhaled by us as we lie in bed. What we don't know, doesn't trouble us – unless we are allergic to it. If we are, however, it brings on an attack of asthma, just as breathing in pollen gives an attack of asthma to those who are allergic to that.

There is also a house mite that lives in damp houses and feeds on the green and black mouldy patches that develop on the wallpaper in such dwellings. Drying out the house and changing the wallpaper usually persuades it to leave.

There are other mites which live in our food cupboards. Did you ever find an old half-used bag of flour and discover that the thing was moving when you looked inside – or, worse, when you had poured it out on to the weighing scales? Well that was the flour mite, which doesn't just confine itself to flour but can spread all around the food cupboard, eating anything it can get into. We are always getting samples of these in to the programme, wrapped in napkins and tissues, with pleas for help. At least I think we are: they are usually so small and decomposed that I have to assume so from the description of their depredations (not being a forensic scientist used to dealing with minute evidence). In any event, the remedy is the same – clean out the food cupboard, put opened bags of stuff into sealed boxes and eat it up fairly smartly. Why do you think 'best-by' dates were invented?

Mind you, flour mites are not the only things you might find crawling round your food cupboard. There is a whole collection of beetles that think the food you buy in the supermarket is specially for them and they particularly like the dry food that comes in packets such as flour, biscuits, spaghetti, dried fruit and even chocolate. The story is the same in each case – the packet has a tear in it or has been opened, then left unused for some time. The female lays her eggs on the food and the larvae hatch out and do the damage. The biscuit beetle, for example, was traditionally the beetle that affected ships' biscuits – really hard tack that had to do the sailors until they next took on supplies in port. No point in being squeamish here. You took the precaution of tapping the biscuit sharply on the table before eating it, to knock the larvae out – unless, of course, you wanted a mouthful of protein with your carbohydrate. They're not unknown on land either. One listener sent in a sample (visible this time, because beetles are bigger than mites) of a beetle she found in a group on the inside of her window. She was not at all fascinated to learn that it was a biscuit beetle and time for a major clean-out and disinfecting of her pantry.

The confused flour beetle has a great name. It's not all that confused when it is selecting your bag of self-raising to devour. The name comes from the way it behaves when disturbed. It runs around until it finds shelter and then it stops, unlike the grain weevil say, which runs around when disturbed and doesn't stop. Now, if I was naming them on their running behaviour, I would be inclined to think that the flour one has a great deal of savvy to stop running when it reaches shelter – perhaps it's the observer that gets confused.

There's also a collection of meat-eating beetles with names like the bacon beetle, the leather beetle and the museum beetle. With the advent of fridges and the disappearance of flitches of bacon from the chimney breast, they are no longer common in houses. They are still around, though, doing the work nature intended them to do, eating carrion and cleaning up the place.

So, bad and all as you may feel your house is, with uninvited guests, the remedy is in your hands. Remove their source of food and – eureka – they'll be gone. This is much more effective than spraying the house willy-nilly with poison, which indeed you may inadvertently ingest yourself – or, worse, paying a pest removal company vast sums of money to poison it for you.

TEACHING TEACHERS

I BEGAN WORK in 1974 in An Foras Forbartha as head of the Biological Records Centre. This was a grand title indeed because I was not only the head, but the body, arms and legs as well – in fact the sole member. I was employed to make distribution maps of our animals and plants so that we would know where everything was and, I suppose, make planning decisions accordingly. However, I had to depend on others to send in records of the Irish flora and fauna, as I could not be out covering the country recording everything and inside making maps at the same time. As environmental studies had only been introduced into primary schools in 1971, public knowledge of wildlife was not great. And people had to be able to know and recognise wildlife before they could send in records of it – so how could I ensure a supply of reliable records?

One way of teaching the public to recognise wild creatures was to run courses for teachers and they, in turn, would pass it on to their pupils. There was a scheme in vogue in the 1970s whereby primary school teachers gave up some of their holidays to undergo training to become better teachers. They did this voluntarily, at their own expense and in return they could claim three days leave during the school year – three days discretionary leave for the five days' holidays that they had given up. And when they took these three days leave during the school year, no paid substitute was provided – their class was taught by their colleagues in addition to their own pupils for no extra charge. Nice one, Department of Education! What other employer could get their employees to undergo staff development at their own expense during their holidays? This was the story in the 1970s and the remarkable thing is that it is still the case. If a teacher wants to attend a funeral or a wedding or have a day off for any personal reason, or even take delivery of a washing machine, the only way is to have the three days squirrelled away.

So by organising a course that met with Department of Education approval I could get teachers to come along and learn about Irish wildlife. Teachers, particularly primary teachers, are a unique constituency. Firstly they are a most tolerant audience. Technical hitches – such as projectors breaking down, rooms which cannot be darkened, power failures, non-appearances of guest lecturers, rain – all are understood and forgiven. All, that is, except a problem with tea breaks. Once tea and coffee (however dire) can be provided at the promised times on the schedules, all is well.

Secondly, it seems that the primary school day is the model for all work done by teachers. This leads to the situation whereby lunchtime on a teachers' course is half an hour only and happens between 12.00 and 12.30 while the whole day ends at 2.30, just as a school day would. As they are paying for this out of their own pocket and attending during their holidays you can't really blame them for applying the maxim, 'He who pays the piper calls the tune.' But it doesn't suit bird life in particular – birds tend to doze and be quiet in the middle of the day after the dawn frenzy.

Providing a teachers' course certainly is an effective way of acquainting teachers with their environment. It gives them confidence to be reassured that knowing the names of creepy-crawlies is not the be-all and the end-all of everything – after all, spiders and squirrels and earwigs do not know their own names but they function perfectly well in spite of this. And, indeed, recognising a species is not a matter of divine inspiration. One does not wake up one morning, knowing the names of all wildlife. They have to be learned painstakingly, one by one. As the names have been imposed on them by us, it actually has been done according to an overall plan, not willy-nilly. Explaining this and showing how a totally unknown flower, say, can actually be named using an identification key is very satisfying – provided, of course, that you have chosen the correct flower, one that obeys the rules and is not the exception. Keys work very well in theory, but there are always some species that are identified more easily than others and some, sad to relate, that are downright exceptions. One of the tricks teachers like to learn is which to choose when showing off to their pupils how proficient they are.

The real problem with teachers' courses is the time of year when they happen. Teachers collapse into a course in the first week of July, exhausted after a hard year's work, delighted to let someone else do the talking, but by the time they get back to school in September, the details of what they have learnt have faded somewhat. I used to think that a course the last week of August would be the business, and I see now that they are beginning to happen in the last year or so.

Ah, yes, a breed apart, primary teachers. Delaying your holidays is one thing, but cutting them short (however long they may seem) and returning to work early and voluntarily is bordering surely on the masochistic.

THINGS THAT STING AND THINGS THAT DON'T – WASPS, BEES AND ANTS

RIGHT, BEFORE WE start, let's get one thing straight. People sometimes find it hard to tell the difference between a honeybee, a bumblebee and a wasp. So here is the definitive statement. Wasps are shiny, not hairy, and have yellow and black stripes. Bumblebees are large and hairy and have stripes of colour, mainly yellow, on their backs. Honeybees are about the same size as wasps but they are easy to recognise – they have a dark brown or black body, thinly covered with beige hairs. There is no yellow on them and you couldn't mistake them for the shiny, stripey, yellow-and-black wasps if you look at them at all.

I must nail my colours to the mast at the outset and state that I am on the side of wasps. They are the victims of bad propaganda, much of which is entirely undeserved. Honeybees are the goody-goodies – symbols of industry and harmony, working away busily making honey for our delectation, pollinating flowers as a sideline and doing all this with harmonious sounds. Yeats's 'bee-loud glade' was part of the idyllic scene immortalised in the poem 'Lake Isle of Innisfree'.

Well, let me put the case for the wasp. Like many of our insect species, wasps overwinter as fertile females, or queens. Only queen wasps survive the winter – all the drones and the workers die off during the first frosts. Come a fine, sunny day in spring, the queen hibernating down her mousehole or wherever she is escaping the winter frosts, wakes up and emerges into the sunlight. She has to get the show on the road by herself, so she needs first of all to find somewhere to live – somewhere suitable where she can rear a large family. She needs space and food.

The ceiling of your garden shed seems ideal, or the hole behind the fascia board, where she can gain access to the attic – anywhere she can attach a nest to some exposed wood, because wood is vital for making the nest. She scrapes off some dead wood, either from your rafters or an outside post or a rotting tree, chews it to a pulp and spreads the pulp in a spherical shape, which she attaches to the ceiling of the nesting site. It resembles nothing more than a paper golf ball stuck to the ceiling with a hole in the underside. Wasps were, in fact, the first paper makers, and the nest is made from paper woven in the most fantastic shapes. Construction continues and eight hexagonal cells are formed inside. An egg is laid in each one and the queen is then very busy collecting food to feed the hatching grubs.

And what does she feed them with? Sugar? – wrong. Nectar? – wrong. What do all baby wasps dine solely on? Insects, that's what. The queen is busily scouring your back garden for greenfly, whitefly, blackfly, anything small enough to be collected and brought back to the ravenous young.

They quickly grow up and develop wings but never become sexually mature, so they are no threat to the queen, although they are all female. They take over the building and feeding duties and the queen then goes into the egg-laying business full-time. Bit by bit, the nest is built up and the queen lays in each new cell provided. Every grub that hatches out has to be fed greenflies, whiteflies and so on from your garden. The queen can lay up to 40,000 eggs in a season. That's a lot of provisioning – and a lot of garden pests got rid of for us.

But what do the grown-up worker wasps eat themselves? No more than ourselves, they are not into baby food. The greenflies *et al* are all right for the young-uns, but adult wasps, like ourselves, have a sweet tooth that must be satisfied. The solution is ingenious and a model of sustainability – they eat the saliva of the larvae. Baby wasps produce very sweet saliva and it gives the worker wasps all the nourishment they need.

Any particular batch of wasps lives six weeks from egg to death in old age and there are many generations in the nest over the summer months. The queen lives for a twelve-month period, hibernating as soon as she is mated and then spending all the next summer laying eggs. By the end of the summer, as you might imagine, she is worn out and her supply of eggs is coming to an end. Time to think of the future. She is able to produce male eggs at this time, which hatch out into stingless male wasps (only the females sting). Some carefully selected female eggs are reared to queenhood. And then, of course, the inevitable happens. The new queens disport themselves shamefully, they are pursued by the males, mating takes place outside the nest, males from other nests are involved too, and next year's supply of wasps is assured. None of the wanton creatures are readmitted to the nest after their high jinks. The males, having performed the one useful task of their lives, are now surplus to requirements and don't survive long. The mated queens find somewhere to hibernate, such as a disused mousehole.

But what of the old nest and the founder queen? Eventually she stops laying and dies of exhaustion, having provided one last egg round. The grubs which hatch out of this final round of eggs are fed, as is customary, by the previous generation and, in return, generously allow them to eat their dribble. But when they grow up they are the last of their tribe. There are no babies to feed – hurrah! – but no saliva to eat either and a lifetime of nearly six weeks stretching before them. They must find sweet food somewhere else.

Every September we become very aware of wasps. They come into our houses, they invade classrooms, they spoil picnics. They have short tongues, so they can get sweet nectar only from shallow flowers. They can feed as well, however, on fallen fruit oozing their sweet contents. And they are also very good at smelling out sweetness; leave an open jar of jam in the garden and you will attract hundreds within minutes. But if we send them the wrong signals, we must be prepared to take the consequences of our actions.

If we have fallen for slick advertising and are washing our hair with shampoo containing apricot essence, or wildflower scents or some such, how can we possibly blame the wasps for becoming confused? They smell the scent of fruit, they come to investigate, they buzz around our heads looking for the sweet food that we have so clearly indicated is there and what do we do? We try to beat them to death, with shrieks that we're being attacked. We go for them with rolled up newspapers, and whack them as hard as we can. And the wasp does what any self-respecting foraging wasp being attacked does – it stings the aggressor. Would you blame it?

Wasps have a sharp, pointed sting, for all the world like a hypodermic needle. Mind you, it's only the females that sting: the sting is a modified ovipositor or egg-laying canal. They can stick it into us, release some venom, withdraw and fly away to sting again. It doesn't take a feather out of them. The same cannot be said for us, the recipients of the stings. The stings are alkaline, so we should rub vinegar on them to neutralise them.

Some people are hypersensitive to wasp stings – having being sensitised by the first one they ever received. What happens is, the sting is seen by the body as a terrible invasion of foreign danger and it produces antibodies against it. When such a hypersensitive person is stung again, and it could indeed be years later, the body's antibodies 'remember' the foreign danger and immediately spring into action to get rid of it, but the antibodies in such a hypersensitive person react out of all proportion. They produce chemicals that can cause anaphylactic shock and kill. Such people may have to carry adrenalin injections (as an antidote) with them for such eventualities, but in the main they keep out of the way of wasps in the first place.

Wasps mainly get in our way in September and October, yet all wasps, at all times of the year, are tarnished with the same brush. As for the discovery of the nest in the attic – which usually seems to happen in autumn when it is the size of a football at least – this leads to apoplexy, to the calling out of expensive pest-removal companies and frantic calls to our wildlife programme. We get more calls about wasps than about any other creature. And in truth all you have to do is hang in there till the first frosts, when all the wasps in the nest die of cold. Wasps do not last in a paper nest in the attic from one year to the next. The old queen dies in September. Her last lot of offspring live six to eight weeks at the most. By Hallowe'en, never mind Christmas, in any half normal year, there will be no more wasps left alive in the nest. And that is the end of the wasps in that particular nest. It is a temporary little arrangement, as it were. Next year's queen will want to start a fresh new nest come spring, not set up home in a smelly second-hand nest. The nest is now all yours.

What you do then is spray it with hair spray to prevent it from breaking – wasp nests are very brittle – and take it down and admire the co-operative building skills of the wasp. Or, indeed, you can even leave it there. Mind you, if the nest is in a good site, plenty of food available in the garden, raw wood around for nest building – in other words a prime piece of real estate – next year's queen may build her nest next door. Really good untouched attics may have five or six wasps' nests hanging down from the beams, one for each year. They will all be empty except for the current model. So just think of the number of garden aphids that these helpful residents have removed from your garden plants over the years – and for free, with no poisoning of the food chain, as sprays would do. Fascinating creatures wasps – you couldn't prefer greenfly?

Bees are also social insects, which means that they too live together in a large, female commune bossed over by a queen. They too can sting, and do, but we have a much more benevolent attitude to them than we have to wasps. They are synonymous with quiet industry and happy summer days. I wonder how many of us realise, when we describe someone as being as busy as a bee, that bees actually die of exhaustion from all the work they do. Maybe their lives are not all sweetness and light.

Honeybees have always been prized by man because of the honey they produce. We only have the one species in this country, *Apis mellifera*, and it is almost entirely domesticated. Some do make a break for it and set up nests in chimneys or hollow trees or hay sheds, but they are one and the same species as the domestic bee, and any beekeeper will be glad to lay hands on them.

All summer long they visit flowers, making a noise not unlike a cat purring – *crónán na mbeach* it is called in Irish, which is more descriptive than merely calling it humming. (Why do bees hum? Because they don't know the words.)

They have the same general set-up as wasps. They have a queen, a fully mature female who does nothing else all day but lay eggs. These are all female and they hatch out to become worker bees. They have the potential to become queens but they are not fed long enough with the top-quality food while larvae, and so they have a stunted development, as it were. They are quite content to work for the good of the hive for the whole of their lives. Bees have several different areas of employment and they work in each of these departments during their lives.

Feeding the young is a very important part of the work of the hive. All larvae are fed a substance excreted from the salivary glands of the workers. This bee dribble is called royal jelly, no less. Ordinary potential workers are fed with pollen after this – which their older sisters collect from flowers and bring back in special baskets on their back thighs. This is a protein-rich food and it's good enough for the babies, who, after all, are going to grow up to be drudges like their older sisters. The older sisters, of course, can eat what they like and what they like is honey. But first it has to be made. This is the entire work of another group of the sisters, who are not on baby-feeding duties. They visit flowers to collect nectar, a sweet liquid deep within the flower, which they lap up with their long tongues. They bring this back to the hive in their tummies to concentrate and store in special cells as honey. As flowers of a particular species open at the same time, they can make varieties of honey depending on the time of year – heather honey, clover honey, apple blossom honey, and so on.

Like anyone else, bees can take short cuts if these are available to them. Beekeepers in Drogheda were amazed at the amounts of honey their bees were making, until they discovered that they were not making it at all but stealing it from Boyne Valley Honey, whose honey they were able to access. Needless to say, this loophole was quickly sealed off and the bees were back to hard graft.

Bees can communicate with each other where the best flowers are by means of a dance – different steps tell how far away the flowers are. I wonder how they told each other to abandon flowers altogether and head for the honey-packing company – and what the atmosphere was like at the dance afterwards, when they had been found out!

There are other jobs to be done in the hive as well. Cells have to be made out of beeswax, and the workers have special wax glands for this. They also have to repair the hive and seal up intruders. Mice, for example, can get into a hive and steal honey. Killing such a robber is no problem, particularly if you have a thousand angry sisters to help you sting it. Soon it lies dead on the floor of the hive. But how do you stop it stinking the place out? The bees cannot physically drag the mouse out, but they can embalm it. Collecting resins and glues from timber is another area of work that bees do, and they use what they collect to seal up the mouse so effectively that it never decomposes or causes further harm to the bees.

So in its lifetime, the bee progresses through all these activities. No wonder it dies of exhaustion after a few weeks, particularly in summer when bees work flat out! And, of course, should she drop dead in the hive, she'll be quickly carried out and discarded by her heartless sisters.

Another difference between wasps and honeybees is that, while wasps' nests only last for a year because, with wasps, the new queen founds a new nest and the old one dies off, bees' nests go on forever. We heard on the programme about a bees' nest found at the top of an old hay barn which had to be removed with the bucket of a tractor. It was so big because it had been there for many years.

Interestingly, the running of the hive is controlled by the worker bees. They make the cells for the queen to lay eggs in and, depending on the shape and size of the cell, the queen will lay male or female eggs. If she lays female eggs in the normal hexagonal small cell, they will be fed royal jelly for only three days and become workers. If the female eggs are laid in cone-shaped cells, they will be fed royal jelly for longer and develop into fully mature females – queens. If the cells are of normal shape but bigger, the queen will be stimulated by the shape to lay male eggs, which will hatch out into drones. How does the queen know in advance it's going to be a male egg? Elementary, my dear Watson! It's an unfertilised one. Although the queen was thoroughly fertilised on her wedding flight with all the sperm she was ever going to need, it didn't join up at the time with her eggs. She can choose whether or not to fertilise the eggs with that sperm as she lays them. Females come from fertilised eggs, males from unfertilised ones. The shape of the cell stimulates the process. And, as it is the workers who prepare all these cells for the queen to lay in, essentially it is they who control what happens in the hive.

If the workers feel that the colony is about to swarm, in other words, if they think the queen will do a runner with half the colony, they make sure that she lays in cone-shaped cells before she goes, and also puts down a supply of suitors. The first new queen to hatch out is instantly on the ball. Her first act is regicide – she visits all the other cone-shaped cells and stings the other queens to death. Effective, or what? She then makes sure the drones are aware of her presence and when she has them suitably aroused, flies off out of the hive up into the air on her marriage flight with the amorous males in hot pursuit, not only from her own hive but from nearby ones as well. The strongest, most daring, best flier and sharpest operator is the successful one, ensuring that the best male genes go forward to the next generation. Not exactly the *survival* of the fittest, as the poor drone loses his life in the process – as do the also-rans. The sisters are delighted to welcome back the new bride, who takes up where her runaway mother left off, in the same hive, but the door is firmly closed to returning drones who, disappointed in love, are now left to starve to death.

But what of the old queen who departed with her swarm? The sight of a swarm of bees is enough to strike terror into the stoutest of hearts. But apparently bees have no interest in stinging at this time. They stuff themselves with honey before they leave and are so full that it is difficult to bend their bodies to sting. But they will sting if forced to, to defend the queen. They accompany the queen who is looking for a likely site to set up a new home. Well-organised beekeepers have an open empty hive just waiting, but sometimes this is not the case and the swarm takes off. It may land in a tree or a shop front or somebody's porch or chimney, causing absolute panic. Beekeepers are very good about going out to such situations, not least because they usually get to keep the new swarm. The earlier in the year the bees swarm, the more time they will have in the new nest to build up a supply of honey before the winter – hence the rhyme:

A swarm of bees in May is worth a load of hay
A swarm of bees in June is worth a silver spoon
But a swarm of bees in July is seldom worth a fly.

Queens only swarm once, so when the swarmed queen is getting old and beginning to lose vigour, the sisters cop on and once more build the cone cells and encourage the queen to lay. The first new queen out this time not only commits regicide on the other potential rivals, but is a willing accomplice to the killing of her aged mother by the sisters when she comes back from her successful marriage flight. No retiring gracefully to the old bees' home, in spite of having had maybe 50,000 children!

When winter comes, honeybees, unlike wasps, do not die off.

They cluster round the queen, feed on the honey they laid down during the good times and have a well-earned rest. Enough of the workers survive the winter to be able to attend to the queen when she starts laying again in spring.

Bees were very greatly valued in Ireland long ago. They provided people with their only source of sugar – there was no sugar cane or sugar beet here then – and so they were very important. Monks, in particular, kept them in monasteries in straw hives, called skeps, and often there were special niches in monastery walls for these. Some of these niches have survived to this day. Of course, alcohol could be made from the honey, and some monasteries were famous for their well-made mead.

Is it true that bees will die if they sting? Well, they will if they sting us. Again, only female bees sting, and their sting is shaped like a fish hook. When they stick it into us, our skin is so tough that it gets caught, and they can't withdraw it – so it tears away from their body, leaving an open wound in their abdomen, from which they quickly die. If they sting softer things, they can withdraw the sting and escape intact. Queens don't die after stinging other queens, quite the reverse actually.

When we get stung by a bee we are left with the sting sticking up out of our skin. The thing not to do is to grasp it, trying to pull it out. This will only pump more of the poison venom in. You should scrape off the sting using a finger nail (or a new euro, if your nails are bitten to the quick). And these are acid stings, so bread soda is the old-fashioned antidote.

Honeybees, both queens and workers, live all the year round, an indication that, however long they have been here, they are not native to these latitudes. Only the mated queen survives in all our other groups of social bees and wasps, so honeybees must have evolved in regions where winter was not cold like here. It is thought that they were brought to these parts by man and were originally native to southeast Asia.

We do of course have native social bees – I refer, of course, to the bumblebees, or humble bees as they were once known. They are big, fat bees, black in colour, with bands of yellow and indeed other colours too, depending on species, across their bodies. They are very hairy and really couldn't be mistaken for either a wasp or a honeybee. These too are social insects. They live together in nests ruled over by a bossy super-female, the queen. Like wasps, they all die out every winter, with only the mated queens surviving. When spring comes, the emerging bumble queen is one of the earliest insects to appear – sometimes one can be seen on a sunny day in late February flying around seeking to get the show on the road. We have several different species of bumblebee here. The ones that most of us are familiar with build their nests in holes in the ground, say mouseholes. People often used to discover them in late summer when cutting hay. Bumblebees don't often sting people, but they can, as any haymaker who has accidentally chopped open a bumbles' nest can testify to.

The queen selects a suitable mousehole (one assumes that the mouse has already departed) and builds a nest out of dried grass and moss – she may even steal the former occupant's bedding. Then she visits what flowers are in bloom at this time of year and gathers nectar and pollen from these. She brings this back to her mossy nest and makes a concoction known as 'bee bread' from it. She spreads this in the centre of the nest, like a disc, and lays up to a dozen eggs on it. She then builds a wax wall, with wax from her wax glands, around the eggs and – wait for it! – she sits on the eggs to keep them warm. She's nothing if not versatile, our queen bumblebee, not like the spoilt queen honeybee who is waited on hand and foot.

Oh yes, and before she settles down to incubate the eggs, she runs up a little wax honey pot and fills it with honey to keep her going during her confinement. She could give lessons to single mothers. After five days, the eggs hatch and the larvae feed on the bee bread they have been so fortunately laid on. They pupate into worker female bees and – you've guessed it – they get lumbered with all the work, feeding all the other babies the queen produces. The bee bread was just a blind to start the operation. The queen does keep control by building the wax cells she needs to lay the eggs in – no being ordered around by bossy workers who decide what she must lay. And so it continues all summer. The honey is made by the workers, who store it in wax pots.

Bumblebees make nothing like the amount of honey that honeybees do – they don't need to, as they won't be overwintering on it. Towards the end of the summer, the queen lays eggs that become drones and new queens are produced by longer feeding with royal jelly. Mating takes place, again a frenzied affair up in the air with lots of suitors in hot pursuit (the flight of the bumblebee!), and then the new queens go off to hibernate for the winter. The old queen weakens and dies and the workers die away. The whole story must begin again the following spring.

A curious thing can happen to a bumblebee's nest. It can be invaded by a cuckoo bee, a different species of bee that looks very like the species she parasitises. Like cuckoos in the bird world, cuckoo bees do not build their own nest but seek out a nest of their chosen species of bumble. The queen cuckoo waits until the first round of workers are hatched out and then she enters the nest. She eats any eggs the bumble queen has laid, lays her eggs in their place, and the worker bumbles have to rear and feed them. Oh yes, and she kills the founding bumble queen. Of course, being a cuckoo bee, she has no pollen baskets on her legs, so she is dependent on the bumble workers to feed her. And, of course, all her children are fully mature males and females, no workers here. So there is really only one generation of them, as the whole set-up can only last as long as the enslaved bumble workers live to feed them. But they have really screwed up the happy bumble home and there is an unexpected empty place at the bottom of the hayfield when haymaking comes round.

Ants live in communes as well and all work for the good of the community. Ants originally had a good press. In the Aesop fable about the ant and the grasshopper, it was the grasshopper who was feckless, whiling away the summer as a guitar-playing layabout, while the good, industrious ant worked away to be prepared for the hard times ahead. This was seen as a good thing. People are not a bit positive towards ants nowadays, though, and seem to have a terrible aversion to them on their property or – God forbid – in their houses.

It all depends on your point of view. Let's hear it for the ant. The ant most commonly complained of to us is a perfectly harmless creature called the garden ant. Like all ants, this is dumbell-shaped insect with a large head and a large abdomen and a very narrow bit in between. It lives with the queen and all its worker sisters in a simple nest excavated in sandy soil. There are no structures in it as in, say, a bees' or wasps' nest. The ants live in a series of chambers and tunnels. The queen has a royal chamber, of course, where she lays the eggs. She can lay one every ten minutes at the height of her powers, when she really gets going, and she can keep this up for up to six years. The workers then reverentially remove the eggs and hatch them out elsewhere. The eggs get great attention from their worker sisters as they develop, being moved about the nest as they grow from eggs to larvae to pupae. They are even brought up to tunnels just under the surface on warm days so that they'll grow big and strong even quicker.

All these young need lots of food and the worker ants forage far

and wide to gather it. Any particles that are small enough to be carried are painstakingly lugged back to the nest to feed the others. If a good source of food is found, the ants communicate this to each other and soon a whole line of them is on the way to collect more. All these ants live underground in small little tunnels, which are just big enough for them to move around in. At certain times in summer the queen lays eggs, which develop into sexually mature adults (unlike the poor workers which are always undeveloped females). Nests at this time of year become like primary schools long ago and are either *buachaillí* or *cailíni*, containing mainly male or mainly female mature adults. During certain weather conditions, these mature adults, all of which have wings, unlike the workers, erupt from the nests and have one glorious abandoned orgy in the air. As well as attracting the notice of hassled humans, all the aerial feeders in the bird world are attracted to the spot – swallows, swifts, even gulls – and there's sex and violence and gluttony and murder all going on at the same time.

Very few ants survive this. It doesn't really matter about the males: once they have done the business, they have no further role anyway. But the successfully mated queens who escape the depredations of the birds, fall to earth and the first thing they do is break off their wings, first one, then the other. You can easily observe this as you sit on your patio with your sundowner. They are then able to squeeze back underground and seal themselves up until spring. They can survive on the reserves supplied by the wing muscles that they no longer need. Good recycling, huh? When spring comes, the female ant starts a colony by laying the first batch of eggs and feeding them with her own saliva. When they hatch out, she has her workers, so she can go into the egg-laying business full time.

So why are people so exercised about them? Well, from the ants' point of view, people are very kind and have modified their homes and gardens to make life easier and better for them. In the first instance, they have removed the damp, heavy topsoil from a portion of the garden and replaced it with nice dry sand and roofed this sand with nice flat patio slabs. Perfect for tunnelling in and building nests – sand is so much easier to tunnel and build a nest in than soil, and the slab roof gets nice and warm, so good for the little growing larvae! And then, this sandy habitat is conveniently placed just beside the house itself, into which access has been much improved by the provision of nice glass double doors, particularly on those hot days when ants are always so starving. And there's always food to be found in the house, lots of tiny crumbs on the floor or on the worktop. Occasionally, the ants even hit the jackpot and find a food cupboard open with tears in the sugar bag, or no lid on the sugar bowl. They have to be careful not to wander into the fridge if it is left open. It gets very cold and dark in there when the door is closed and they cannot move for the cold, even when the door is opened again. Ants are sure that the humans must be grateful to them for carrying away all the things that they spill on the floor and the patio.

But the humans are not, they are so not grateful. They hoover up the poor industrious creatures, not caring how many babies are left to starve to death. They put down horrid ant poisons in the form of dusts sprinkled round the doors where they get in, not seeming to care if it blows on to their own food. And, all the time, they do not seem to realise that they brought the problem on themselves by constructing the sand-based patio that screamed 'come and live here' to the ants. And I am supposed to provide an instant solution to all this on the radio! These ants don't even sting, for heaven's sake – so what's the problem? We are lucky we don't live in Africa, where we could have to cope with army ants that can kill humans if enough of them sting together, or termites that could easily gobble up the expensive wooden decking that is such a feature in your

garden. Nobody forced you to have the patio, get rid of it if you really can't abide the poor ants.

We do have other sorts of ants here too. If you examine your roses you may find that they are host to lots of greenflies, particularly now that we seem to be having such mild winters that they are not wiped out from one year to the next. If you just stand and gaze at the greenflies you may notice that there are ants walking up and down the rose stems as well. These are actually tending and minding the aphids like cowherds do in Africa – I kid you not. And what they get from the aphids is a sweet secretion, a delicious liquid pooh called honeydew. They feed on this, so it is in their interest to mind the aphids and keep nasty predators, such as ladybirds, away from them so that their dinner and tea are secured.

Remember the picnics we had by the seaside in the summers long ago, when the sun always shone? Well, do you remember sitting down on the nice soft grass on the back dunes in your togs to eat your food (or indeed do other things)? And you weren't there five minutes when you were attacked by pissmires – great big ants – and these fellows really stung. We should be grateful that this species hasn't taken up residence in our sandy patios – yet...

CHAPTER TWENTY SIX

MALIGNED AND MISUNDERSTOOD – WHO'D BE AN INSECT?

THERE ARE MANY creatures with which we are all familiar that have an undeservedly bad reputation. The wasp is a bit different: it's a victim of false advertising – our false advertising that is, luring it with smells of food that we don't deliver – but wasps can and do sting, so I suppose they do something to warrant their bad press.

But what did an earwig ever do to anyone? The very mention or sight of one causes people to shudder involuntarily. Yet the only crime, as far as I can see, that it commits is that it doesn't look too lovely to some of its beholders. I wonder what we must look like to an earwig? The nerve of us 'Johnny-come-latelies' in the evolutionary stakes, having the temerity to accuse a species that has been on this planet for millions of years longer than us, of not being good-looking enough to justify its existence! When did good looks ever come into it? Earwigs are exemplary mothers who look after their young – which is more than can be said for the much admired feckless butterfly or dragonfly. Alas, such exemplary behaviour does not improve its lot in the affection stakes. Beauty is all.

The English name earwig is a corruption of an earlier English name. If you so much as give an earwig a passing glance, never mind examine it closely, you will notice that it has two appendages protruding from its rear end. These are not to pinch people with, but are a help in the mating process. These were considered to be a sort of wig that covered the lower abdomen of the insect, and so it was named, in the normal accepted English of the time, arsewig. (The wheatear, a bird of our uplands, was called, in the same vernacular, white-arse because of its white rump.) When prissiness overcame the official use of the word, 'arse' was changed to 'ear', thus giving us earwig (and white ear – later wheatear) instead.

But I digress. Earwigs are fastidious creatures. Their preferred food is flower petals. They are particularly fond of dahlias and have the unnerving habit of exiting from such flower arrangements across the white tablecloth, when guests are assembled at dinner. That is if they weren't in the tablecloth in the first place. They quite often come in on clothes from the line – the smell of Lever Brothers' products must convince them that the washed clothes are flowers.

How do they get on to the line? Why, they fly of course. Earwigs have wings, which they keep folded up under their wing cases. It has been reckoned that they have to be folded forty times to fit in there, and the earwig uses its abdominal forceps to help with the folding. It's obviously all a lot of trouble, because they don't fly very much.

Listeners to the radio programme have decided views on earwigs. Many are convinced that they go into your ears. One listener regaled us with a story of his summer holidays in the 1950s in a rented house by the sea in County Louth. It was idyllic and the sun shone the whole time as it always did in those days when we were young. It was all great, except for the cotton wool in your ears. Cotton wool, in your ears, on holiday by the sea? Why, of course, their mother put cotton wool dipped in Vaseline into their ears every night to keep out the earwigs. And it worked!

Where did such a belief come from? Why do many people think that earwigs will go into their ears and deafen them by biting their eardrums? Well, it is true that earwigs like tight spaces. They like to feel a surface on their back at the same time as beneath their feet. A good place to hunt for them is in the dead, hollow stalks of the hogweed in autumn. It is conceivable, I suppose, that if you lay on the ground with your ear correctly positioned one could come calling, but they would soon retreat from the average waxy, hairy ear hole. They certainly wouldn't bite your eardrum, or force their way into your skull – unless, of course, you keep dahlia petals in there. But it is much more likely that the belief comes from the name, which, of course, as already explained, really has nothing to do with ears.

The sawfly is another misunderstood insect that graces our postbag in numerous matchboxes during August and September. Usually it comes with the words, 'What is this and how do you get rid of it?' Mind you, it does look ferocious. It is a large black-and-yellow stripy insect with a long needle-like ovipositor protruding from its bottom. It is about 3cm long and the horrified correspondent is usually convinced that it is a hornet.

We don't have hornets in this country and I must say the first time I saw a hornet, in France, I was quite disappointed. It was merely a large, reddish wasp – no terrifying protruding sting, no sudden savage attack. Mind you, I didn't provoke it.

The sawfly, or to give it its proper Latin name *Urocerus gigas*, really looks the business. However, the protruding needle from its abdomen is not a sting, but an egg-laying tube – an ovipositor – and

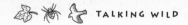

it is long because it is a mini-fretsaw. It files a hole into timber and then lays its egg into the hole. The ones we get here in Ireland have a black ovipositor, which means that they are the northern European subspecies.

Usually it is people who have moved into new houses who find them. What happens is that the eggs are laid into the timber in Scandinavia. An egg hatches out and spends two to three years as a larva inside in the hole, eating the timber. After this it pupates and emerges as a fully mature sawfly – two wings, enormous eyes like any member of the fly family, the black-and-yellow stripes and, if it is female, the fearsome-looking ovipositor. Of course, by this stage, the timber has left Norway or Sweden and become the roof trusses of your new home. You have moved in and are just in time to welcome the emerging adult insects. Of course, they'll do you no harm – they don't sting – but here again appearances are everything and they are promptly dispatched, in a matchbox, and sent in for their five seconds of fame on the wireless. Don't do it! Admire the creature instead and open the window and let it off. (The fact that it finds itself in Ireland instead of in Sweden will be punishment enough for it.)

And while I'm at it, can I put in a word for the *deargadaol* – the rove beetle. Again, its various names indicate the odium with which it is regarded, the devil's coach horse being another of its common names. This large, black beetle comes out at night to hunt for smaller insects and indeed it is partial to the odd earwig or two. (That should improve its popularity stakes in certain quarters.) The rove beetle is a belligerent fellow and faces up to his enemies, no matter how large. It is a big beetle, maybe up to 5cm long, and it has the disconcerting habit of facing its perceived enemy and cocking up its tail over its back to make it look more fearsome. If you pick it up it is well able to nip your hand and cause you to release it pretty smartly.

In the old days in houses with flagstones or indeed earthen floors it commonly walked around houses at night. On suddenly being interrupted by us, instead of running away, it would face the perceived danger with its tail cocked over its back. It was considered to be the height of bad luck in certain parts of Mayo to see the *deargadaol* in this position. Mothers used to shield children's eyes from such sights. Devil's coach horses are still around and turn up occasionally in the postbag for identification. They can give you a nasty nip if they are still alive, as they quite often are when you empty them out of the matchbox. But they have well earned their place in your garden as a voracious feeder on slugs and other invertebrates, which, if left unpredated, would be feasting on your precious plants.

SEX AND THE
SINGLE PLANT

THE AIM OF every living thing is to reproduce. If you don't reproduce and pass on your genetic information to the next generation, there's an end to all that talent that is uniquely you. Living things that don't reproduce become extinct. There are two blueprints for reproduction – sexual reproduction and asexual reproduction. Asexual reproduction isn't much fun. A piece of the adult breaks off and grows into an exact copy of the parent – cloning in other words. Sexual reproduction, on the other hand, requires that cells from two different parents fuse, producing slightly different offspring with genes from both. So the old joke is true – the essence of sex is the loss of genes! (Try saying it out loud if you don't get it.)

Plants have been reproducing successfully for millions of years, at least the ones we see today have. And they employ every trick in the book to make sure that this continues to happen successfully.

There are two major stages to effective reproduction, as anyone who ever gave birth to a baby knows. The first stage is getting pregnant, which itself requires particular skills and talents. The second is producing the healthy offspring, which will grow and flourish and, in turn, go on to reproduce.

It is exactly the same in the plant world. The first stage is called pollination and a plant 'gets pregnant' when the male pollen lands on the ripe female part of the flower and fertilises the egg. In the animal world, which includes us, this is easy enough (in theory anyway). Animals can move, so the two sexes can physically get to each other to do the deed. But plants can't move. Fertilising yourself is not a good idea from a genetic point of view, and – for this reason – usually the male and female parts of the same flower are not ready at the same time. So the male part has to get the pollen to go to a ripe female flower without being able to deliver it itself. (The human equivalent might be if, in order to continue the human race, men had to send sperm in the post to likely females and hope for the best.) The plants do in fact use postmen – at least some of them do – and the postmen they use are messengers from the insect world.

Now we all know that bees pollinate flowers, and some of us realise that flies, butterflies and moths do it as well. But they don't have a meeting every morning where they decide to go and pollinate a few flowers just for the hell of it. In fact, insects don't know they are pollinating flowers at all. They think they are going for a drink, just as if a flower was a pub and they were popping in for one. Most insects smell the perfume of the open blooms and visit the flowers to drink the nectar, which is cleverly stored in a little sac way down deep at the bottom of the flower. To get to it, the insect has to put its face right into the flower and stretch its tongue all the way down to the nectar. Of course, in doing so, it gets its face covered in pollen. It's not really much of a pub, it only has one drink to serve the customer, so off the insect goes again, on a pub crawl to the next flower, where it repeats the performance. In doing so, it introduces the pollen from the previous flower to this next one, where the female part may be ripe this time, and so pollination takes place. By the end of a long morning's flower-crawling, the insect will have a very dusty face and may have left behind some very satisfied flowers indeed.

The only insects that are interested in pollen *per se* are the pollen eaters, who collect it and bring it home in baskets on their legs – the bees. To all the others, it is a nuisance that gets between them and the drink. There are, of course, a few flowers that attract insects with more than just nice smells and sips of nectar. The arum lily smells horrible to our noses, because it promises feeds of raw meat to visiting meat-eating flies, in order to get pollen from one lily to another.

The bee orchid takes the performance a step further. The petals of this orchid are arranged so that it exactly resembles a certain species of bee. When the male bee sees the flowering bee orchid, it thinks it is a female of its own species. So it approaches and attempts to mate with it. As it gets into position, the pollen of the orchid is released in such a way as to stick on to the forehead of the amorous bee. Much disappointed at the lack of enthusiasm with which it is received, the bee flies off seeking another mate with the pollen fixed firmly on its head. At the next flower the pollen is in position for action if the female part of the orchid is ripe – never mind the bee and his desires. I suppose the bee must eventually find a female bee, not an orchid, or the whole thing would come to a sudden end. It is interesting, with such a complicated procedure in place, that these orchids are also self-fertilising. There must be a need for a default option.

Not all flowers have petals. After all, petals are only there so that the insects will notice the flowers and come calling. If you are not depending on insects to act as a go-between, then there's no need to spend all that energy getting dressed up in lovely petals. Many flowers that depend on the wind to pollinate them have no petals because, after all, the wind cannot see. The most obvious of the wind-pollinated flowers are the catkins that come on hazel, willow, poplar and birch early in spring, long before the leaves come on the trees to get in the way of proceedings. These catkins shamelessly flaunt their pollen on long, dangly catkins and the wind blows it away like yellow talcum powder. In a way, this is a profligate waste of resources: all this genetic material is just flung into the air in the hope that some of it will land on receptive female catkins. And the wonder of it is that it does. Grasses, rushes, sedges and such plants all go in for this kind of carry-on too, though a bit later in the year.

The problem, from our point of view, is that there is such an abundance of pollen around in May and June that we breathe it in as we walk through grassy areas. Pollen has a very hard silica coat and even though each grain is tiny, in some people's air passages the grains cause an irritation, which manifests itself as hay fever. The other thing about this pollen is that it goes everywhere as dust. If it lands in bogs, it becomes incorporated in the turf. So by looking through a microscope at turf of a known age – say 2,000 years old – we can see what pollen is there and thus know what wind-pollinated plants were growing at the time. This technique is called 'pollen analysis'.

Anyway, by whatever means, boy meets girl and the eggs are fertilised. This will enable them to swell to form seeds, and some plants may have many eggs and thus many seeds. These are all potential new plants. The aim of the parent plant – like many parents – is to get the seeds as far away as possible so that they can settle down and raise large families of their own. Thus there is no point in a hawthorn tree or a holly tree just dropping all the seeds on the ground underneath. There will be no space in the ground for them to put down roots, because it's all taken up already with the parent tree's roots. Also there will not be enough light under the tree for the seeds to send up leaves. So it's not a good idea to drop all your seeds on the ground around you if it's immortality you're after. You need to bribe someone to do the job. Insects and creepy-crawlies are a bit small for tree seeds – you couldn't imagine a bee or a butterfly flying off with a haw. No, the job specification is for the bigger boys – the birds and the mammals. And they have to be bribed into doing this, as they don't see themselves as foresters and gardeners.

So the trees giftwrap their precious seeds in a sweet, juicy coat and ensure that the coat is a bright shade that can easily be seen, such as red, or shiny black, or yellow. Think of a holly tree, or a blackthorn tree with sloes, or a mountain ash, with gleaming berries in autumn sunshine. The birds flock there and feast hungrily. And inside each berry they gobble whole is a hard seed. After a feed of ten or twelve berries, the seeds begin to accumulate rather uncomfortably in the bird's tummy. How to get them out? Think about it. Did you ever see a bird up a tree coughing up berry stones? No, they go right through and are voided at the other end, together with a handy bit of manure to help the seed on its way as it germinates and grows. And, of course, all this is accomplished well away from the parent tree. Every autumn some gourmet bird which feasts on elderberries in my locality perches on electric wires above where my car is parked and festoons the car with elder seeds and fertiliser in an effort to start an elder wood on the roof. But elder is a very common tree in all our hedgerows, so many of the seed-bearing poohs must in fact bear fruit.

So if the hedges are full of berries in autumn, it's not really a sign that there is a hard winter ahead and that provision is being made to feed the birds. Much more prosaically, it is just a reflection of the fact that the previous spring was a good time for pollination. The insects were on the ball, the wind blew enough pollen to the right places, and there was enough moisture and sunshine all summer long to swell and ripen the berries. But none of this can possibly indicate what winter will be like. If it's harsh, well, the hedge has a good supply of food for the birds, and if it is mild, sure the birds won't need the berries.

What about nuts? If a squirrel eats hazelnuts, or a jay gobbles up an acorn, surely that is the end of it. Nothing is going to grow from squirrel droppings. Surely this is a silly thing to do, making the seed itself the food, instead of wrapping it in food. Have trees such as beech, oak, hazel and chestnut lost the plot? Well, hardly, seeing as there's no shortage of them. They rely on the overproduction principle that so much wildlife subscribes to. Go out and look at an oak tree in autumn that's covered in acorns. If every single one of those grew into a new tree and did this every year for the lifetime of the oak, as did the acorns of all its offspring, we'd soon run out of space on the planet. Much is wasted from the tree's point of view, but enough nuts get to germinate all the same. The tree relies on creatures such as squirrels, field mice or jays and rooks collecting the nuts and taking them away to store for eating later. Perhaps they'll drop one, or forget where they put it, or even not survive the winter at all, leaving the cache untouched and ready to germinate when spring comes. Nut-bearing trees can afford to sacrifice most of their offspring for the common good, that of successfully passing on their genes to the next generation.

Of course, there's a collection of plants that can't be bothered with all this truck of bribery and fancy packaging. They are into aerodynamics. Put wings on the seeds and get the wind to blow them away for free. This works very well, as anyone who ever had to remove miniature sycamore trees from gutters and chimney pots

will verify. Ash are masters of this method, as are lime, birch and most of the conifers, which have winged seeds inside their cones.

In fact, so good are plants in general at getting rid of their seeds and starting up new generations, that to take them on is a mug's game. Seeds will germinate in any bare patch of soil as gardeners and farmers know only too well. It's very hard to impose your own will on nature without taking mean advantage and poisoning it with weedkillers.

NATURE'S WEIRDOS – FUNGI

MUSHROOMS BELONG TO a really weird group of organisms – the fungi. While these are definitely not animals, they are not plants as we know them either. They do not make their own food, but cadge it off other organisms. So they are usually not green in colour, as they contain no chlorophyll. That green patch of damp mould in the corner of the bathroom is a fungus all right, but the green colour comes from the spores, which are just ready to shoot off and colonise another nice damp piece of wallpaper.

Amazing to think that such unpromising material can be the source of so much pleasure. One fantastic thing that certain fungi can do is change sugar into alcohol. (All we can do, for all our sophistication, is change the alcohol into water!) Yeasts have been known to have this ability since the time of Noah. All they need is a sugar source – such as honey or grape juice, or less obvious ones like fermented grain – and drinks, such as mead or wine or beer, can be made from their endeavours. These yeasts float around freely in the air all the time, just looking for a sugar source to convert to alcohol.

One of the most exotic of tastes is said to be that of the truffle. It has been described as aphrodisiacal, food fit for the gods. Truffles are fungi that spend all their lives underground. They are associated with the roots of certain trees and can only be detected by smell. However were they discovered in the first place and who ever thought of eating them? Who but the French and the Italians! Black truffles are found in the Périgord region of France and white truffles in Albi in Italy. People use poodles and pigs to sniff them out, and then sell them for astronomical prices in the local markets.

We are not known to have truffles in Ireland, so imagine our surprise one day when we got a call on the programme from a listener who had found a white egg-shaped truffle under the ground. Was it a first? Could it be a truffle? Truffles had never been recorded for Ireland, but maybe nobody had looked – we are not noted as a race for our adventurousness in eating wild food. We couldn't wait to get our hands on it.

A white egg-shaped thing duly arrived, cosseted and carefully wrapped. It was a fungus, definitely, but there certainly was no heavenly smell. There was really no smell off it at all. Eventually, having poked and prodded at it for a while, I cut it in half to see if this would help with the identification. According to the identification books, white truffles should be all white on the inside too. This one, however, had a dark green line forming a circle in its centre and it certainly didn't smell any more heavenly than it had in its entire state. In fact there was still no smell off it. Back again to the mushroom books and consultations with mushroom experts. The only truffle ever described for these islands was a thing called the summer truffle, which was green on the outside, white on the inside and had a warty skin and a sweet smell. Ours was white on the outside, with a green line on the inside and had a smooth skin and no smell. Sadly, not a truffle.

It actually turned out to be a baby stinkhorn, *Phallus impudus*, which looks like an egg in its youth, but quickly bursts forth from the egg to attain the shape so graphically described by its Latin name, and the smell which gives it its English name. The green line becomes a slimy spore-bearing cap on the top and its disgusting smell quickly attracts flies, who land on it and take off again with the spores on board to spread the fungus far and wide. A few of these in your garden and you would be convinced that your septic tank was acting up. Food of the gods? Heavenly aphrodisiac? Not on your Nellie!

Fungi will grow anywhere they can get a bite to eat and they are not particular in their dining habits. Athlete's foot, an annoying itchy and sore condition of the feet, is caused by a fungus that just loves sweaty shoes and smelly areas between toes. Ringworm is caused by a fungus which grows on the skin of the scalp and can cause bald patches. Fortunately, these conditions can now be treated with modern fungicides, but in the old days these conditions were much more common than they are now and 'cures' of all sorts were peddled. Thrush is also caused by a fungus, a bad yeast in this case, which loses the run of itself when the normal body bacteria that keep manners on it are destroyed by our use of antibiotics.

Our homes are havens for all sorts of fungi. Many species live in timber. After all, that is their job in the real world – breaking down dead timber and recycling the nutrients there. How are they to know that the timber in your window frames or rafters is off limits? One of the most spectacular fungi that can attack your timber is dry rot, although if you come across it in your house, you will hardly be in a mood to marvel at its growth patterns. It grows in massive sheets and splits the timber into squares as it goes, completely ruining any structural strength your timber had. It can even travel over masonry with no timber there at all to get to the next bit of timber. Getting rid of it requires ruthless amputation of all timber that's even adjacent to it. By comparison, wet rot lacks flamboyance. Oh, you wouldn't welcome that in either, but it is slower and less dramatic than dry rot and somehow doesn't strike such terror into the heart of the beholder.

Dead wood can host a great variety of fungi, all with the general aim of breaking down the timber by growing on its nutrients. One particular species, the honey tuft fungus, which grows inside hollow trees, is luminous and glows away as it spreads slowly through the softening timber. One can only speculate as to why it is luminous. (Is it afraid of the dark?) In a world without electricity and light pollution, when people travelled at night on foot or on horseback, such phenomena were noted and marvelled at. We tend not to travel in the pitch darkness nowadays and so are not really aware that luminous fungi exist.

So it was with complete incredulity that we listened to the tale of the luminous flying object seen by one of our listeners one dark night as he returned home in a completely sober condition. Seeing something like that would sober you up quickly, right enough. Piecing the story together and getting a description of the flying object, it became apparent what it was. It was an old owl, which spent its days asleep in a hollow tree obviously infected with honey tuft fungus. It had lived there so long that the fungus was all over its feathers, so when it came out at night it glowed in the dark. Our informant was obviously made of stern stuff. A lesser man could have dined out for months on tales of ghosts and banshees.

Fungi have also been implicated in deaths on a truly biblical scale. Ergot is a fungus that grows on rye. Its fruiting bodies replace the grains in the ripened rye and so can end up in the harvested grain. When bread is made from this, people end up eating ergot without being aware of what they have done and the results can be truly awful. One result is a condition known as gangrenous ergotism. After eating the infected bread, sometimes as soon as twenty-four hours later, the limbs become covered with swollen blisters, which soon develop into gangrene, and nails, thumbs, fingers, toes and even whole limbs become mummified and fall off. Death quickly follows. In another form of the disease, the first symptom is a tingling, burning sensation in the hands and feet. This was referred to as 'holy fire' in the 11th and 12th centuries. People then had no idea what caused these conditions, which could suddenly affect a whole parish, and they ascribed it to a plague sent by God as a punishment to sinners. It was particularly common in France, where rye was much grown for bread. The first account dates from AD 857, when 'a great plague of swollen blisters consumed the people by a loathsome rot, so that their limbs were loosened and fell off before death'. In 1722, Peter the Great of Russia could not undertake his planned campaign against Turkey because 20,000 of his cavalry died at Astrakhan after consuming ergot-contaminated rye bread. Nasty stuff.

Ergotism became much less common after 1772, when a failure of the crop led to a famine in France and they changed from growing rye to growing potatoes. You could say they jumped out of the frying pan into the fire, because the potato did not stay free of infection from fungus for long either. As we know only too well in this country, in 1845 a new fungal disease of potato was sweeping Europe – potato blight. This fungus, carried by the wind and thriving in the muggy, wet conditions of a typical Irish July, grew on the leaves of the potato plant, quickly reducing it to a black rotten mass. It didn't confine its attentions to the leaves, but rapidly invaded the whole plant, particularly the potato tubers, which rotted as they lay in the fields. People recognised it only too well, so they didn't eat the infested potatoes and get an awful disease as the people who ate the ergot-infested rye bread, did. They just had nothing to eat at all, because the potato was the only food they had, and 1 million of them died from hunger and famine-related disease during the ensuing Great Famine.

Mind you, horrible diseases weren't the only thing ergot in rye gave you. Clever women early in the middle ages recognised that judicious use of it would bring on labour pains and contractions and induce childbirth – surely a welcome potion in a world where pethidine and epidurals were unknown. I'm sure some of them were branded as witches and burnt at the stake for their efforts, particularly if they used the ergot to induce contractions at a very early stage in the pregnancy, causing abortions. Ergot, as we now know, contains a whole cocktail of drugs, one of which is closely related to LSD and could induce hallucinations. There are those who unkindly attribute the 'voices' that spoke to Joan of Arc and inspired her to lead the French against the British, to eating mouldy rye bread infected with ergot.

Other fungi are well known to contain hallucinogens, and some of these occur in Ireland. The fly agaric is a bright-scarlet mushroom that appears in late summer in areas where birch trees grow. It also grows commonly in Lapland and the Lapps noticed that when their reindeer ate it, it affected their central nervous system, causing them to be highly overactive and to make giant leaps up in the air. (Obviously Santa Claus keeps a supply for Rudolph and the rest of the team.) The Lapps further noticed that the urine of such reindeer was also hallucinogenic if drunk. (How do people discover such things? The mind boggles.) However, the fly agaric also contains other substances, which are poisonous to humans. These occur in varying amounts from one mushroom to another, so, while eating one might bring on elation and vivid dreams, a different one might induce a death-like sleep (maybe that's how people ended up being buried alive!), or in extremely unlucky cases death itself follows ingestion.

Getting high on fly agaric isn't worth the risk unless you're Rudolph.

Magic mushrooms are the liberty caps that grow on lawns and pastures and which fruit in autumn. They are small toadstool-type mushrooms, yellowish brown in colour, which look not dissimilar to many other small grassland species. The problem really is being sure of your identification – getting the wrong one may hasten your demise. Mushrooms are one of the few categories of wildlife in this country that contain specimens that can kill you outright with no known antidote. It's not for nothing that some of the deadly *Amanita* species have names such as the death cap, panther cap and destroying angel. In fact, if you are trying out wild mushrooms, it's always a good idea to leave a sample of each on the mantelpiece for the state pathologist, to save him having to cut open your stomach to establish cause of death.

Still, I'd better not leave you with the impression that fungi are the enemy. Alexander Fleming was growing colonies of bacteria in a culture in a laboratory to study their characteristics. Some of them got contaminated with the green fungal moulds that are always floating about as spores in the atmosphere. Instead of sighing and throwing them out, he looked at them and noticed that anywhere the fungus was growing in the dish the bacterial colonies were kept back a considerable distance. It was as if the green fungal mould was causing the bacteria to retreat. And so it proved. He called the bacteria-destroying substance produced by the fungus 'penicillin', and modern medicine took a giant leap forward. We cannot imagine living without such antibiotics today and, despite there being a whole range of them available, penicillin is still of paramount importance.

Still, I don't recommend licking your green mouldy bathroom wallpaper if you have a sore throat. Better give the pharmacist his prescription fee.

THE **ONES**
ST PATRICK MISSED –
AMPHIBIANS AND **REPTILES**

WE HAVE A very poor collection of wild amphibians and reptiles in Ireland – only three amphibians and one reptile are definitely on the list, with the possibility of another. It all goes back to the end of the last Ice Age, when Ireland became an island before many of these slow-moving creatures got as far as our shores. Reptiles in particular like warm, sunny climes, so they were in no hurry northwards. They wanted to be absolutely sure that the weather was going to last, so no snakes and only one lizard got here under their own steam. The amphibians were no speedier and we have only one definite native species – the smooth newt. A great deal of doubt is attached to the status of the other two, the frog and the natterjack toad.

But to begin at the beginning. What is an amphibian? It is a creature that can live in two domains – in water and on land. It is entirely dependent on water for reproduction. The eggs it lays have no protection against drying out and they hatch into gill-breathing, swimming tadpoles. But, as they develop and grow, they sprout legs and lungs, lose the gills and can leave the water and live on dry land. However, they do not lose their ability to live in water, and in winter can even hibernate for months at the bottom of ponds. Needless to say, the lungs are no good to them for breathing at this time, so they obviously have a further trick up their sleeves. They can also absorb oxygen through their skin, and this is actually more important than breathing through the lungs. On land they need the oxygen from both the lungs and that absorbed by the skin to keep them going; whereas in water, during hibernation, when their metabolic rate has slowed down, the skin alone is enough.

Amphibians are considered to be very primitive animals, one step up from fish. However, this was a vital step, because it enabled life to emerge from the sea and become established on dry land. They first emerged from the sea during the Devonian period – 400 million years ago – and have been around ever since. So think of that the next time you look at a frog. Humans are hardly three-quarters of a million years here on the planet and we behave as if we owned the place!

The most common amphibian in Ireland is the frog. This species is the common frog and it occurs in every county in Ireland. Although it is very abundant here, it is scarce enough on mainland Europe, and so it is protected under the Wildlife Act, which makes it an offence to interfere with it or destroy its habitat, and it can only be captured and bred under licence. This has led to the situation that, if a school wanted to put frogspawn into a fish tank to observe the emergence of tadpoles in the classroom, the teacher had to apply to Dúchas for a licence. So every spring Dúchas was deeved and demented with applications to keep frogspawn in classrooms around the country, when truth to tell, the species is under no threat here at all. Naturally, there has been an Irish solution to an Irish problem – a general licence to breed frogs in classrooms, but nowhere else – has been granted by Dúchas to the Department of Education and Science for schools. At least common sense prevails and the law is still respected.

Growing them in fish bowls and tanks is easy enough if a few points are remembered. The condition of the water affects their growth. After all, they don't know that they are in a fish bowl – all they can sense is that the water is getting stagnant, running out of food and waste products are increasing. No point in developing any further if there's going to be no grub. So, to keep the development moving smoothly along, the water should be changed regularly, preferably with water from the pond where the spawn was collected. Secondly, tadpoles are carnivores and eat the tiny animals in the water that surrounds them. They can be nasty little cannibals too and eat each other if times get hard. Another reason for changing the water regularly, or you may end up one Monday morning with only one very fat tadpole with a smug, satisfied smile on his face.

Avid gardeners should make every effort to encourage frogs into the garden, as they are very partial to snails and slugs and, in some cases, these constitute a quarter of the diet. They also eat caterpillars, centipedes, woodlice, beetles and flies, so if you have a down on those levels of the food chain, get a frog or ten.

They, in turn, are part of the diet for lots of other animals such as hedgehogs, rats, stoats, otters and birds such as herons and grey crows. They are even part of the human diet but not, of course, of ours here in Ireland. In France and Belgium they regularly eat a different species which doesn't occur here – the edible frog. They are so addicted to the taste of the *grenouille* that they will eat the poor common frog in early spring when the edible one is still in hibernation. And by all accounts, you'd have to be a very specialised gourmet to tell the difference between the legs of the edible frog and those of the common frog when they are reclining on your plate in a pool of garlic butter.

Not every predator of frogs enjoys every morsel, and sometimes the leftovers from the frog feast are unrecognisable as ever having belonged to a frog. Sometimes in autumn people find a whitish jelly-like substance on the ground which they can't recognise. The old wives' explanation was that it was left behind by a shooting star, but the truth is much more prosaic. It is an uneaten part of a frog, which its bird predators don't like – the glands of the oviduct. These glands, on exposure to moisture, swell up and burst, and decompose into masses of jelly. As there will be no other trace at all of frog nearby, there is no clue as to where they came from. They must taste horrible if herons take such definite action to avoid them.

What colour is a frog and can you foretell the weather by looking at its colour? Well, only sort of. There are three different types of pigments in a frog's skin and each type makes a different colour: black, yellow/orange and white, and sometimes red as well, are all made by these pigment-making cells, and the colour of the frog on any one day is a result of which of these colour-making cells are being stimulated most. Moisture, darkness and low temperatures stimulate dark colours, while dryness, light and high temperatures favour light colours. So black frogs are a sign of rain, or at least reflect the fact that it has been cold, dark and raining for some time already. A period of bright, dry, sunny weather gives us yellow frogs. But as frogs can change their colour in two hours if conditions change, how can looking at a frog's colour tell us anything about the future? It only reflects past weather that we, of course, know already.

Interestingly for a species so common and so well adapted, the common frog is not thought to be native to this country. The story is that there is no Irish word for it, only frog. No less an authority than Pádraig Pearse pronounced this; yet in the dictionaries they give *loscán* as the word for a frog, and the oracle, De Bhaldraithe's dictionary, gives another word, *lispín*, which was commonly used for the frog in Sligo, when it was Irish-speaking. Of course, the frog wouldn't have to have been here since the Ice Age to have an Irish name. After all, the magpie, which arrived in 1676, is the *snag breac*, the hedgehog is the *gráinneog*, and the rat was called after those who brought it – *francach* (although whether these first rat-bearing strangers actually came from France itself cannot be scien-tifically proven – they hardly owned up to the crime).

Robert Lloyd Praeger, an eminent, Victorian, Irish naturalist, was particularly interested in the frog and its Irish status and he has gathered together the story in his book, *The Way That I Went*. Much of the history of animals in Ireland goes back to a researcher (if that is the word) from the 12th century, one Gerald of Wales, Giraldus Cambrensis, a gullible lackey of King John who came here, appar-ently on a fact-finding mission. He enquired about the status of Irish wildlife and dutifully wrote down and recorded everything he was told, apparently believing it all, as he enters no caveats. It would seem the more he wrote down, and thus gave importance to, the taller the tales he was spun. He thus reports verbatim the 'fact' that nothing venomous brought here from other lands could survive in Ireland. Serpents shipped over specially to Ireland were found to be dead and lifeless as soon as the middle of the Irish Sea was crossed (they would have been handy for the map-makers!). According to old Giraldus, when toads were deliberately brought here and put on Irish soil 'they immediately turned on their backs and bursting their bellies died, to the astonishment of many who witnessed it'. And we think it is only the English tabloids in Ireland that are given to exaggeration! Nevertheless, in Giraldus Cambrensis' time in Ireland, didn't a frog turn up near Waterford to the astonishment of all! Even though this was 1187 and the Normans had landed in 1169, the king of Ossory, who happened to be in Waterford at this time and beheld the frog, was able to 'forecast' that this previously unknown 'reptile' portended the coming of the English and the subjugation of the Irish nation.

There is no further account of frogs here at all until the end of the 17th century (being the portent of such gloomy news was obviously too much for the Waterford frog). At that time, some Trinity students, no doubt doing a baseline study, found that we had no frogs in Ireland and thought this was contrary to the order of things. So, to improve upon nature, they introduced the frog from England to a ditch in College Park, from whence frogs spread all over Ireland. So think of this the next time you behold a common frog – its ancestors were graduates of Trinity College, no less. Another thing to blame the reign of William of Orange for.

What is the truth in all of this? One way of verifying the authenticity of our native species is finding old bones in archaeological deposits. There was great excitement in 1979 when amphibian bones were found in a grave in a Megalithic cemetery in Carrowmore, County Sligo. Surely this was proof that the owner of the bones was around in Megalithic times, 5,000 years ago. Recent zoological studies on the bones established that they were the bones of the common frog, but radiocarbon dating puts them at only several hundred years old, not several thousand. The frogs were a recent visitor to the grave. And no frogs' bones more than several hundred years old have ever been found here, despite research in the area, so the old tales may well be true.

Certainly it is commonly accepted that it is a sign of bad luck if a frog comes into the house, and that one way of curing a toothache is to place a live frog in the mouth. I can't see too many dentists being put out of business by that practice and I can't really recommend it, as there are glands on the skin of frogs that are distasteful if not downright poisonous.

But what of toads? The common toad is abundant in Britain, but does not occur here. How would you know which was which? The common toad, when fully grown, is of a similar size to a fully grown frog, so size is no help. The majority of toads are brown and warty, but you can get brown warty frogs too. No, the simple difference is in the way they move. Frogs are marvellous hoppers, whereas toads can hardly hop at all and walk around the place looking for food. I think it might strike us as odd if we encountered walking 'frogs' – odd enough, at least, to phone up the radio programme. We get reports, after all, of red frogs or early frogs or late tadpoles, but never of a big, brown, warty, walking 'frog'. They only seem to be encountered by Irish people camping in France.

We do, however, have a species of toad in Ireland – the natterjack toad. This toad has a very distinct yellow line down the middle of its back and runs, very definitely runs, not walks or hops, but runs. It only occurs in west Kerry, and lately in The Raven in Wexford, so I think you'd probably recognise one if you saw it and not mistake it for a frog. Again, a mystery surrounds the origin of this creature in Ireland. It only lives in the wet areas of sand dunes by the sea – in dune slacks. It lives in burrows and so must have sandy soil which it can excavate and ponds where it can breed, both of which constitute a dune slack. Natterjacks were first recorded in 1836 in Kerry in Castlemaine harbour in the *Magazine of Natural History* by the naturalist Mackay, who had just then got around to recording the fact that he had first seen them there thirty-one years earlier. But just as Columbus didn't really discover America, since the Native Americans knew it was there all along,

so too did the native Kerry peasantry (as the Victorian gentleman Mackay described them) know all along about the 'black frog' as they called it. At that time the natterjack toad only occurred in a circle around Dingle Bay from Inch to Rosbeigh, and the story went that a collection of them were brought here by a ship which discharged them on to the shore.

Before the mind begins to boggle at the thought of a group of natterjack toads booking a passage to Kerry, remember that, in those days, ships used loads of sand as ballast when they were sailing with a small amount of cargo, and dumped the sand when taking on a full load. So it is not inconceivable that a ship sailing into Dingle Bay to take on a large cargo could have rid itself of sand ballast taken on in another country where there were natterjack toads hibernating in burrows in the sand. The natterjack is a western European species, occurring in England, France, Spain and Portugal, and indeed further east in Belgium, Holland, Denmark and Germany as well. There could well have been trade from any of these countries to Dingle Bay.

These toads are habitat specialists and as the quality of their coastal habitats declines, because of drainage, erosion and invasion by sea water, so too do their numbers. At their height they were found well away from Dingle Bay near Cahirciveen and at Caherdaniel, but a careful survey carried out in 1971 failed to re-find them. They have since been introduced to State-owned properties at Derrynane near Caherdaniel and to The Raven in County Wexford, and the introductions have proved to be successful.

It is to the credit of the Castlegregory Golf Club that they appreciated the danger the toads on their golf course were in, when sea water breached their breeding ponds at the end of the 1980s. They created special breeding ponds for them in the vicinity of the ninth hole, and they have been thriving ever since. It's not often I find myself praising golf clubs for their sensitive approach to wildlife, but credit where credit is due.

The other amphibian we have is the newt. Is there any possible explanation for the expression 'as pissed as a newt'? It's no more appropriate than the expression 'drinking like a fish' (Fish do not gulp down great mouthfuls of water – you'd always have to be replenishing the fish tank if that were so. They take water into their mouths to pass out over their gills and not to drink, although it looks to us like drinking.) The species of newt we have in Ireland is the smooth newt. There are two others species as well in Britain, but only the smooth newt made it this far. It is like a small lizard in looks, as it is long and narrow and has a tail. In fact the Irish word *earc* is used for both species, the newt being the *earc sléibhe* (lizard of the mountain), while the lizard is *earc luachra* (which could be either the silver lizard or the lizard of rushy places).

Another name for the newt is the mancatcher, and it is implicated in Irish superstitions. It was thought that if you fell asleep out of doors with your mouth open such a creature could jump in and live in your insides. Indeed such a fate befell a king of Munster and the creature inside him caused him to have an enormous appetite, so that he caused famine wherever he went. In the end, a holy man had to be sent for and his remedy was to fry rashers of bacon and dangle them in front of the king's mouth. The creature, maddened by hunger, leapt out to get at the rasher, and then the king closed his mouth and the country was saved. (Great hunger can in fact be caused by large tapeworms in the intestines, so maybe this fanciful tale had its origins less romantically.)

The newt is widely distributed in Ireland and it can be seen on land or in water. It hibernates on land and returns to ponds to breed. The eggs are laid singly and are attached to vegetation or sticks in the water. They hatch out into newts, but they do not lose their tails like frog tadpoles do. They are able to grow a new tail or even a new limb or part of the head if they have the misfortune to be injured. Sometimes this regeneration process loses the run of itself and newts with two tails or extra legs are found. No wonder they feature in stories and myths!

Lizards are a different class of animal entirely. These are reptiles, a much more advanced group than the amphibians, and one which took over the world for millions of years in the form of dinosaurs. They quickly succeeded the amphibians in evolutionary terms, appearing on this earth a mere hundred million years after the amphibians evolved. They first appeared during the Carboniferous era, 300 million years ago, and have been around ever since. Dinosaurs, the most famous of all the reptiles, ruled the world from about 200 million years ago until 65 million years ago, when they got their comeuppance when the earth was struck by a meteorite plunging it into a nuclear winter. Reptiles, which are cold-blooded creatures needing the sun to warm them, were at a disadvantage in these conditions, and the warm-blooded groups – the birds and the mammals – had the opportunity they were waiting for. What the creatures of today's world would be like, if it were not struck by that meteorite, we can only postulate. We'd certainly look different anyway, if we were here at all.

This country is not noted for its extremely warm climate, so it is not a haven for reptiles. The only one that got here before Ireland parted company with mainland Europe was the viviparous lizard and it only got here because it had a nud in the race and got off to a flying start. The viviparous lizard doesn't lay eggs like most reptiles, which depend on the ambient temperature being high enough to hatch them out – some hope during wet, cold, Irish 'summers'. Instead, it keeps the eggs within its body until they hatch, because it would be too cold for them outside, and so seems to give birth to live young – hence the name, viviparous, which means having live young. It gets the heat it requires by sunbathing and basking in such sunshine as is available in what passes for a summer in this country (much as we do ourselves indeed). As a result, this species has a greater tolerance of the cold than do egg-laying lizards, such as the sand lizard, which is confined in these islands to the very south of England. Our species, the viviparous lizard, occurs as far north as Lapland and Archangel in Russia.

This lizard has been recorded from all around Ireland. It has a coastal distribution where it occurs in warm, sandy areas, but it occurs inland quite extensively and has been known to breed in boggy areas. There is a certain amount of confusion between it and the newt, when seen on land. The lizard does not go swimming – trying to keep warm is what it is doing lazing about on rocks. It is bigger than a newt too – females can grow up to 17cm, whereas newts are put to the pin of their collars to reach 10cm. If seized roughly by the tail, the lizard can shed it and grow another, although the replacement will never be as fine as the original. It pays for its superior evolutionary status to the amphibians by confining its regeneration talents to tail replacement – no new legs or extra digits here.

But, in spite of being well aware that there are no snakes in Ireland, because St Patrick banished them, you may be taken aback some fine, sunny, summer's day down in the Burren to see what looks for all the world like a bronze-coloured snake sunning itself along with you on the rocks. Do not forswear blue smarties for life – your eyes do not deceive you: you are looking at a reptile called a slow worm. Mind you, it is neither slow nor a worm, nor indeed a snake; it is, in fact, a legless lizard. When disturbed it can move with consid-erable rapidity, gliding, almost flowing, along in a most amazing manner – but they are not snakes, honestly! They have eyelids, which snakes don't, and a broad, flat, feebly notched tongue and, of course, they can't bite and poison us. They are native to Britain and at some time in the 1960s they seem to have been introduced to the northeastern end of the Burren (no doubt causing St Patrick to spin in his grave). The slow worm was first noticed in the early 1970s and identified definitively in UCG (now NUIG) in 1977.

Although they can live in the wild for over thirty years, and in captivity for up to 60 years, we do know that they are increasing and multiplying in the Burren and that it's not the same one that is being seen over and over again. As long ago as 1988, a young one with two adults was seen, and by now they are colonising this wild rocky habitat, which apparently suits them. Their diet consists of worms, spiders and especially slugs, of which they are particularly fond and will eat in preference to any other food, all things being equal.

Someone else, playing God, introduced the green lizard to the Burren in 1958 when fifteen were released. But not having too good an idea of what they were at, they picked a most unsuitable species. These lizards are native to the countries adjoining the Mediterranean, and they must have got some shock the first summer they spent here! They struggled gamely on for a few years and were last seen in 1962, but they did not breed or become established here, probably because the summers were not hot and dry enough.

Introducing species that are not native into Ireland is not a good idea. They come here in isolation, without any of the checks and balances that prevail in the country they naturally colonised, and can cause great upset to the food chain. Mink, grey squirrels, zebra mussels, rhododendron, the salt-marsh grass *Spartina* – they have all been introduced here in recent times and have lost the run of themselves, to the disadvantage of the dispossessed, native species

with which they were in direct conflict. It was the introduction of pigs and rats to the island of Mauritius that spelt the end for the poor dodo, who had had no such ground predators to cope with before. (So why is it that describing someone as a dodo somehow implies that they are stupid and won't move with the times when the real stupidity belongs to the humans who didn't know or care how the natural world works?)

CHAPTER THIRTY

PISEOGA AND FOLKLORE

IRISH COUNTRY PEOPLE were well acquainted with the wildlife they shared their every day lives with – not surprising in a country that had such a large proportion of its population as rural dwellers engaged in agriculture. The people observed and understood a lot about the life around them, but there were many things that they observed for which they did not have an explanation, given the state of scientific knowledge at the time. So it is no wonder that supernatural explanations were offered to account for things that could not be understood.

Birds in particular feature in many of these explanations. After all, birds can fly, although they are heavier than air, and so can come and go as they please, obviously with their own agenda in mind. We know what we consider to be normal behaviour, so anything outside that is viewed with suspicion as it may indicate that they know something we don't.

Birds coming into the house are generally not welcomed. It is widely believed that if a robin comes in, then there will be a death in the family. If an owl comes in, it must be killed, no less, as it will otherwise fly away with the luck of the family. The bird most likely to come into the house is the jackdaw, which falls down chimneys from its nest. No supernatural bad luck is attached to this, apparently, as this is an understandable occurrence (although anyone who ever had to clean up a room after a jackdaw has been flying around it for some time, will have no doubt but that they have been visited with the height of hardship and bad luck).

There is much folklore attached to the robin and how it got its colouring. Christianity has got its version accepted, and stories abound that the red colour is caused by the blood of Christ. In one version, the robin (at that time, apparently, an entirely brown bird), attempted to help Jesus on the cross by plucking out a thorn. Jesus' blood splashed on the robin's breast, colouring it red. In another story, when the soldiers were chasing Jesus to catch him and kill him, drops of blood on the path marked the way Jesus had fled. The brown robin sat on each drop, mopping it up, as it were, and so the soldiers lost the trail, and the robin is red to this day.

There are also older stories about the robin's red colour. These refer to the robin as the bringer of fire, a valuable gift in very old times. The burning brand marked its breast causing the red colour. In any event, the robin is a goody, and anything causing harm to it will itself suffer harm. Cats that kill robins may even lose a limb. Killing or even caging robins brings bad luck to the humans who do so, while boys who rob robins' nests will get sore hands.

On the other hand, the wren is not so highly regarded at all. Christian tradition labels it as the telltale, the one who betrayed St Stephen by flying in the face of the guard who was sleeping as Stephen tried to make his escape. So this is why it gets its comeuppance on St Stephen's Day. Indeed, Irish history continues to malign the wren. It bounced up and down on the drums of the Irish army when it was planning a sneak attack on Cromwell's soldiers, the story goes, thus alerting them in advance. In another version, it is the Williamite army that is being warned by the perfidious drumming of the wren, while yet a third version has it that it was the Danes who were so warned. Anyway, the wren was already known to be a sneaky bird from way back in the days when all the birds were having a competition to see who was the king. He who flew the highest should be king. The eagle, as we know, flew higher than all the rest and when he was exhausted and could fly no higher and was about to declare himself king, the wren, who had been hiding in the feathers of his back, flew up in the air above the eagle and claimed the kingship. In some versions of the story there was a rematch to see who could go the lowest and again the wren cheated by going down a mousehole.

In any event, there was a great tradition of hunting the 'wran' on St Stephen's Day in Ireland. A wren was captured and brought from house to house by a group of performers dressed in disguise. Originally, there were particular characters in the group: a man dressed as a woman, and a character called Jack Straw, and particular lines were chanted or sung. This visit by the wren-boys was welcomed and refreshments were given. At the end of the day, the wren was buried beside the house that treated the wren-boys best. Of course, there were variations on this all around the country but, in general, it was only men and boys who did it, not women. Interestingly, this custom only occurs south of a line from Dundalk to Donegal town. It is virtually absent in Ulster, where the houses were traditionally visited by mummers who came before Christmas, with no wren or any other bird. Apparently, as you might have guessed, the tradition is far older than Christianity and long pre-dates the death of poor St Stephen.

It goes way back to the days of celebrating the return of the sun after the winter solstice. It belongs to the category of rites which have as their object the banishment of evil. Allegedly it was brought to Ireland by Mesolithic people, who came from the Mediterranean through France and built gallery graves here. A different group of Mesolithic people settled in Ulster and built what are described as horned cairns. They had no wren folklore in their tradition – theirs was an eagle culture – and this accounts for the lack of wren-boy tradition in Ulster.

Mind you, wren stories are not the only ones which originate so far back. Swan traditions go back to the early Bronze Age. In those days, the swans that people would be familiar with were the migratory swans, the whooper and Bewick swans. These overwintered in Ireland, but left in spring to return in autumn with new families. It was thought that they embodied the souls of virtuous maidens and, indeed, that they could turn from swans into women. There are various stories about men finding beautiful women bathing in lakes. All goes well, children may even be born, but the one thing the husband must take great care about is never to let her have her original cloak, the one she wasn't wearing when he found her bathing in the lake. Why the men in these legends never destroy the thing in the fire is beyond me, because invariably at some stage the woman finds the cloak, puts it on, turns into a swan and flies away.

Swans had beautiful singing voices and in many cases anyone who heard them fell under a magic spell when time passed with great rapidity. The Children of Lir were turned into swans by their jealous stepmother Aoife, but she left them beautiful singing voices. They lasted until the Christian era, in time to hear the Christian bell and to be baptised and go straight to heaven. Lots of stories based on Tara involve swans. King Eochaid wagered a hug (or something) with his wife Etaine in a game of chess against Midir and lost. When Midir came to Tara to claim his hug, there was great security around the whole place. Undaunted, Midir clasped Etaine to him and they both rose through the smoke hole and flew away as swans. It was nine years before Eochaid got her back (that learned him)! Etaine's grandson, Conor, not aware of the family story – or maybe only too aware of it – was into hunting swans, until one fine day a flock he was chasing landed and turned into armed men who told him that it was very wrong to kill birds. They also told him if he walked naked to Tara carrying only a sling and a stone he could become king. Which he did.

There are also various stories about Cú Chulainn and swans, mostly, I'm sorry to relate, about slaying them or tying them with silver chains.

The mute swan was considered a royal bird in Britain. They were very highly thought of as food, and the earliest record of ownership is for the year 966 when King Edgar gave the Abbots of Croyland rights over stray swans. This is taken to mean that the Crown was claiming ownership of swans by that date, because if strays could be distinguished, then swans must have been marked in some way. The first reference to the swan as the 'royal bird' is from 1186. By 1553 there were about 800 registered swan owners in the fens of East Anglia alone. They were given an individual swan mark to put on the bill of the swan signifying ownership. Anyone caught stealing a swan was in deep trouble, even stealing a swan's egg brought with it the punishment of a year and a day in jail as well as a fine.

Do they sing just before death – the swan song? The story goes back to Aristotle. The swans sing, according to him, not in grief but for joy that they are at last going to meet the god Apollo whose birds they are. But there is thought to be a basis in fact for swan song. Whooper swans have a very long, looped trachea which enables them to whoop. When they were shot, the air in the lungs and air sack would take a while to escape through the trachea and, in doing so, would generate some musical notes. But I wonder – they certainly didn't have guns in the time of Aristotle.

Another migratory bird, the swallow, has lots of fables told about it. Close up you can see that a swallow has red coloration under the chin and it too has been implicated in ancient tales of the arrival of fire. It apparently brought it from the heavens and the smoky dark blue of its plumage shows that it grabbed the burning brand from a fire. In Ireland they were called devil birds, as were swifts. The name comes from the fact that they fly around very fast and, in the case of swifts, shriek a lot and live in church steeples. They were of great use in medicine. In the belly of a swallow there was believed to be a stone which, if acquired from a swallow's nest at the August full moon, would cure epilepsy, blindness and stammering. A case of the twittering bird being used to cure diseases it resembled – sympathetic magic. There is a 1692 recipe which is a cure for falling sickness and sudden fits that calls for the following ingredients:

> Fifty swallows bruised in a mortar, feathers and all
> One ounce of caster powder
> White wine vinegar
> Sugar

The poor swallows! On the other hand it is great good luck to have house martins build nests on the outside of your house, and you must under no circumstances remove them.

The swallow is not the only bird to provide a cure for blindness. The owl, as you might imagine, with its keen sight, has a role to play there too. Eating owls' eggs cured blindness, particularly if they were charred and powdered. In ancient Greece the owl was the bird of Athene, the goddess of wisdom, and so some of the wisdom rubbed off on the bird, giving us the wise, old owl. Athene's nemesis was Dionysius, the god of revelry and ecstasy. So it doesn't take long to figure out that excesses caused by following Dionysius can be cured by Athene's bird. Therefore owls' eggs dissolved in alcohol cure drunkenness and alcoholism, while salted owl flesh was a remedy for gout, a disease thought to have been brought on by too liberal a bending of the elbow.

In Ireland, we only have two resident species. The barn owl, white, ghostly silent, flying at night and with a terrible screech, is the progenitor of many ghost stories and indeed of the banshee herself. The long-eared owl, another night-flying species, spends its days standing still on a branch up against a tree trunk. It is well camouflaged because its plumage matches the tree trunk so exactly that it is very hard to spot. However, if you did see one and it was awake and saw you, you could get it to twist its own neck by walking round and round the tree. It would move its head to follow the movement and so wring its own neck. This species mustn't have passed the aptitude test when being chosen by the goddess Athene. The real explanation is that owls have binocular vision and so have very flexible necks. If you walk in a circle around an owl, its head will turn with you through 180 degrees. Then it will turn its neck back almost 360 degrees and resume watching you. It moves the head so fast that many people don't notice that it flicks its head around and they think that the bird will twist its head clean off.

Owls, because they came out at night, were also associated with witches, so an owl nailed over the barn door would protect from the evil eye.

Eagles have always featured in folklore. There are eagle gods in the legends of Babylon and ancient India, and the eagle was sacred to Zeus and Jove. Roman legions carried eagles on their standards. It is one of the four beasts of the Book of Revelations, which were assigned to the four evangelists. While Mark got the lion, Luke the calf and Matthew the beast with the man's head, the eagle went to

John, and so it appears adorning the lectern in our churches from which the word of God is read.

Eagles were very common in Ireland in olden times, both the golden eagle and the sea eagle, and many placenames derive from them. Giraldus Cambrensis described them as being very numerous when he visited here at the end of the 12th century. They were disliked by farmers, who accused them of carrying away their lambs, and the numbers were decimated by poison and shooting. The story is told of the eagles that nested on Slieve League in County Donegal. They were known to be there and were tolerated by the locals until the time of the Great Famine. People were so starved then, that they died of hunger out in the fields looking for food. The Slieve League eagles, out scavenging for food, came across human corpses and took bits of them back to their nest to feed the young. One man was so disgusted at the sight of human limbs in the eagles' nest that he took a torch to them and burnt the nest. It was not bad enough that the poor unfortunate people had died of hunger, but the final indignity of ending up as food for eagles was a step too far. Eagles became extinct altogether in Ireland during the first two decades of the 20th century. They have been re-introduced to Glenveagh, in County Donegal, as a millennium project and five survived their first winter.

CHAPTER THIRTY ONE

WHY DID **GOD** MAKE **RATS**?

AT THE END of a talk I gave once on the mammals of Ireland I asked, as usual, if there were any questions. I was quite taken aback to be asked, 'Why did God make rats? What good are they? What are they for?' The whole attitude was that anything that shared the planet with us had to confer some benefit on us by their presence and the questioner was at a loss to see any possible redeeming factor in the rat. The truth is that evolution has been such a ruthless selector that any species that isn't perfectly adapted to its surroundings is overcome and made extinct. The question should have been, 'What are humans for? What good are we?'

Rats, like any other animal, only do three things – they spend their time eating and drinking, resting and sleeping, and breeding. A plentiful supply of food and drink means that they can get on with the other two activities. The more food we make available for them – and they eat a very Catholic diet – the greater the numbers there will be. We were plagued with rats long ago because of our filthy habits, particularly because of carelessness in disposing of our waste in cities. The rats acted as dustbin men, the sewage disposers, the eaters of any food we had that was not carefully secured from them. That's why God made them – to punish us for our dirty habits!

Any animal population is controlled by the amount of food available to it. We do not have a million robins in our garden because we only have enough food for a pair. The infestation of bluebottles dies away when the jackdaw carcass they are feeding on becomes picked clean. If you are a species that has only one food source, if that food runs out, you're snookered. Pandas could soon become extinct (there are only 200 of them left in the wild in China) because they can only eat bamboo and the bamboo forests are being cleared because the Chinese want the land for agriculture. Pandas can eat nothing else, so the future, as things stand, is grim. On the other hand, an adaptable species like the magpie can eat a whole range of food. If one thing runs short they can eat something else. They can adjust to the circumstances; they can survive environmental change.

Man is the supremely adaptable species. For much of our existence we were hunter–gatherers. We had to move around continually looking for food. There was no great plenty and our population was low, controlled by available food. When agriculture was first invented by humans 10,000 years ago, our world population was only between 2 and 20 million. There were more baboons on earth than people. We had taken maybe 500,000 years to reach that population level.

But being the only species that could make food appear for us gave us the edge over everything else. Eight thousand years later, by AD 1, we had between 200 and 300 million people on earth. In another 1,500 years, it had doubled again, to between 400 and 500 million. It took just over 300 years to double again, reaching 1 billion in 1820.

Growing enough food to feed everyone was working. People had huge families, one every year the mother was able to reproduce. But such large families suffered from disease and illness. Disease-carrying bacteria and viruses could wipe out whole communities. People died early, in their forties and fifties, from an accumulation of things that wore them out. But then we discovered how to cheat death, at least for a while. Great medical discoveries, such as vaccinations, antibiotics and sterile medical practices, enabled people to live longer. The world population began to rocket. If it took only 300 years to double from half a billion in 1500 to 1 billion in 1820, it took less than eighty years for another half billion of an increase. By 1900 we had 1.6 billion people on earth, by 1950, 2.5 billion, and by the year 2000 the world population had reached 6 billion. With no shortage of food overall (although not equally distributed in all parts of the earth) and with huge medical advances to prolong life, what is there to halt the continued increase? China, with its own population at over 1 billion, has tried a one-child policy, without a great deal of success or support from the rest of the world. No wonder there is no room for pandas!

Because of our own history, lack of food in the 19th century and of money to buy it in the first half of the 20th, our population is completely at odds with world trends. Our lowest population since the 1700s was reached in 1961, when we had merely 2.8 million people in Ireland. It had increased by 1 million by the end of the 20th century. Isolated as we are by our island status from world population movements, we somehow feel that the fact that the world's population has quadrupled in the last hundred years should not affect us.

Is it inevitable that, as we increase in numbers as a species on earth, we leave less and less space for other creatures, and begrudge them the space they do have. If we are so intelligent, is it beyond our wit to realise that this earth will not function with just one dominant species plus the thirty crop species and the fourteen

animal species that, in the main, feed it?

It is estimated, from habitat studies, that we have between 5 and 15 million species on earth, not counting microorganisms – although, as we have only identified and named 1.8 million of these, we cannot be at all sure. One thing we are sure of is that we are making them extinct at a rate not seen since the time of the dinosaurs. Some estimates figure that we are making 25,000 species extinct annually. They are all here for a purpose, and the world won't work without them. So even if we don't like the look of some of them, even if we cannot work out what they are for or why they exist, it should be evident that they have a right to be here.

Adaptable species can adjust to a changing environment; those that can't adjust fast enough become extinct. This does not mean any particular animal scratching its head and deciding to become vegetarian because there are no rabbits around anymore. What it means is that there is so much variation in that species that somewhere there are one or two that are not so affected by the changing conditions. They can still reproduce and have offspring that are also suited to the new, changed conditions. It happens all the time among insect pests of crops. There are always a few that are hardy enough to survive the sprays and, over time, they build up numbers that are immune to the insecticide. We develop a new spray to get those and the procedure happens all over again. It is the same with bacteria that cause disease. We zap them with antibiotics. But, whether through not finishing courses of tablets, or taking them when we merely have a viral infection like a cold that can't respond to antibiotics anyway, we are now seeing the rise of antibiotic-resistant bacteria. It is interesting that, in spite of all these efforts, we have not succeeded in making extinct a single species of disease-causing organisms. (Even in the case of smallpox, which is said to be eradicated as a disease, we had to keep the bacteria in laboratories – and now we're worried it will fall into the hands of terrorists.) Yet, because of habitat destruction – another name for direct competition between man and wildlife for space and food – we have made more than 200 species of large mammals and birds extinct in the last two centuries, and unknown numbers of invertebrates.

We are changing our world all the time. We are damaging the ozone layer and letting in ultraviolet rays capable of causing cell mutation. We are causing global warming by increasing the amount of carbon dioxide and methane in the atmosphere. We are depriving water bodies of oxygen because of our careless disposal of organic waste. We are interfering with food chains everywhere by making certain species extinct. We are setting the scene for non-adaptable species to become extinct and for adaptable ones to mutate and change. How do we know that the ones that are left won't see us off too?

What to do? It's very simple really. Self-interest, if nothing else, should tell us. We have to leave a space for wildlife. We have to realise that all parts of the food chain are necessary. We cannot make life untenable for one section and then wonder what happened to the rest of it. We really have to believe that other creatures are entitled to be here. We have to realise that rarity indicates that the rare creature is just hanging in there and any further slight change will see it off. Roadways are not delayed because they cross the habitat of an endangered snail, just out of bloody-mindedness. The snail is rare and only occurs here and not in adjoining areas, because somehow this place has a little bit extra that the surroundings have lost. The motorway will obliterate all that. Is that so impossible to understand?

Or is it simply that we don't care if we send the environmental bill to our children (it may not even get as far as our grandchildren)? After all, what did posterity ever do for us?

BIBLIOGRAPHY

Armstrong, E, *The Folklore of Birds* (Dover; London and New York) 1970.

Burton, J *et al*, *The Oxford Book of Insects* (Oxford University Press; Oxford) 1974.

Chinery, M, *Field Guide to the Insects of Britain and Northern Europe* (Collins; London) 1973.

Chinery, M, *Garden Wildlife of Britain and Europe* (Harper Collins; London) 1997.

Fairley, J, *An Irish Beast Book* (Blackstaff Press; Belfast) 1984.

Fitter, R (consultant ed.), *Book of British Birds* (Reader's Digest and AA, Drive Publications; London) 1969.

Gleed-Owen, C, F Marnell *et al*, "Origins of the Natterjack Toad *Bufo calamita* in Ireland" Bulletin of the Irish Biogeographical Society (**23**) 1999.

Hayden, T & R Harrington, *Exploring Irish Mammals* (TownHouse & CountryHouse Ltd; Dublin) 2000.

Kelly Korky, J & R Webb, "Resurvey, Biogeography and Conservation of the Natterjack Toad *Bufo calamita* in the Republic of Ireland" *Bulletin of the Irish Biogeographical Society* (**23**) 1999.

Mc Neill, J *Something New Under the Sun* (Penguin Press; London) 2000.

Mackay, J T, "The Natterjack *Bufo rubeta* occurs wild in Ireland" *Magazine of Natural History* (9) 1836.

Marnell, F, "The Distribution of the Common Frog *Rana temporaria* in Ireland" *Bulletin of the Irish Biogeographical Society* (23) 1999.

Mitchell, E & M Ryan, *Reading the Irish Landscape* (TownHouse & CountryHouse Ltd; Dublin) 1997.

Ní Lamhna, É, *Provisional Atlas of Amphibians, Reptiles and Mammals in Ireland* (Irish Biological Records Centre, An Foras Forbartha; Dublin) 1979.

Ní Lamhna, É et al, *An Air Quality Survey of Cork City* (Irish Biological Records Centre, An Foras Forbartha; Dublin) 1983.

Ní Lamhna, É et al, *An Air Quality Survey of the Greater Dublin Area* (Irish Biological Records Centre, An Foras Forbartha; Dublin) 1988.

O Connor, J & P Ashe, *Irish Indoor Insects* (TownHouse & CountryHouse Ltd; Dublin) 2000.

O Sullivan, P, *Irish Superstitions and Legends of Animals and Birds* (Mercier Press; Cork) 1991.

Phillips, R, *Mushrooms and other Fungi of Great Britain and Europe* (Pan; London) 1981.

Praeger, R L, *The Way That I Went* (Figgis; Dublin) 1969.

Ramsbottom, J, *Mushrooms and Toadstools* (Collins; London) 1953.

Roberts, M, *Spiders of Britain and Northern Europe* (Harper Collins; London) 1995.

Roinn Oideachais, *Ainmneacha Plandaí agus Ainmhithe* (Oifig an tSoláthair; Baile Átha Cliath) 1978.

Smith, M, *The British Amphibians and Reptiles* (New Naturalist Series, Collins; London) 1964.

Smith, T (ed.), *Complete Family Health Encyclopedia* (British Medical Association, Dorling Kindersley; London) 1990.

Stapleton, L, M Lehane & P Toner (eds), *Ireland's Environment: A Millennium Report* (EPA; Wexford) 2000.

Uí Chonchubhair, M, *Flóra Chorca Dhuibhne* (Oidhreacht Chorca Dhuibhne; Baile an Fheirtéaraigh) 1995.